HAWKEYE ADVENTURE

THE FLAG OF IOWA

OFFICIAL SEAL OF IOWA

STATE BIRD – THE EASTERN GOLDFINCH

IOWA'S FLOWER – THE WILD ROSE

Hawkeye Adventure

by

Bernice Reida

Ann Irwin

Graphic Publishing Company, Inc.
Lake Mills, Iowa

Foreword

Hawkeye Adventure is based on the observation that Iowa became a great state because of the influences brought in from the outside. As Iowa reached a point of maturity, the movement reversed itself, and Iowa began to contribute to the world.

The first influence was topographical. The fertile soil, the rolling terrain, the forests and streams, the rugged beauty of the hills are an inheritance from the glacier period.

The first tie with the outside world came with the explorers. The French were the first to bring to the history of Iowa stories of the daring adventures of the white man. Iowa was touched and influenced by the Old World as the French carried out their idea that the best way to gain control of the New World was to spread themselves along the great waterways: the Great Lakes, the St. Lawrence, and the Mississippi.

The exploration of the Missouri River was the result of events far removed from Iowa. Napoleon's need for money combined with a fear of the British Navy influenced his decision to sell Louisiana to the United States.

The pioneers who came to Iowa had to face the hostile Indians and a hostile environment. The location of the first homes around the forts was necessary for protection against the Indians. This was an enemy that could be faced and conquered. The hostility of the weather was more elusive. As the pioneers battled the elements and accepted the lot that became theirs, a sturdy, stoic type of people evolved. It seemed as though the law of compensation were at work. If the weather could not be depended upon, the people could be.

The pioneers brought with them the ethics and deep religious faith of many groups. As such groups as the Mormons, the Amish, the Quakers, and the Mennonites made their contributions, a pattern of high morality settled down over the state.

It is little wonder that the ideals symbolized by John Brown found sympathy within the state, that the Underground Railway could find its way through Iowa, and that George Washington Carver could find colleges within the state where he could make real his dream of an education.

These two men mark Iowa's transitional period. Up to this point the state had been absorbing. It reached a moment of maturity when the idealism of John Brown became the battle cry of the North and the experimentation of George Washington Carver began to benefit the entire nation. Iowa had begun to contribute to the world.

The pattern continued to reverse itself. In the field of politics, an Iowa boy became President of the United States. In the wars, Merle Hay in World War I and the five Sullivan brothers in World War II became symbols of Iowa giving her man power for the nation. In the field of the arts, Meredith Willson, Grant Wood, MacKinlay Kantor, and Paul Engle are examples of Iowa becoming a place of culture.

As the last half of the twentieth century ushered in the Space Age, James Van Allen took Iowa to a rendezvous with a new era.

Iowa had come into her own.

Any Iowan can feel justifiably proud as the patterns of the past link with the challenge of the future.

Table of Contents

UNIT I

In the Beginning

History stretches back into the past. If we look far enough into the past, we come to a time before there were any written records. This period is called prehistoric. In order to piece together the forming of the earth and the story of early man, scientists must study the land and any traces of man's existence.

Geologists, who study the history of the earth, have been able to divide the early history of Iowa into ancient periods, trace the glaciers that covered Iowa, and determine what made Iowa into the kind of state it is today.

Archeologists, who study the remains of ancient civilizations, have been able to reconstruct the appearance of Iowa's prehistoric man. By studying weapons, tools, and utensils, they have pieced together information about his culture.

Progress during this prehistoric period came very slowly. Through the years, men found shelter from the weather and protection from animals by living in caves. He learned the uses of fire as a source of warmth, protection from beasts, and later, as a way to cook food. He learned the use of animal skins for clothing.

Early man was a wanderer. He found that seeds could be planted and made to grow. Taming of animals assured him of a source of food and clothing. When man learned these two things, he settled down to live in villages. Early man probably had some kind of religion. The manner in which he buried his dead—with tools,

1

weapons, and even a food supply—suggests a belief in a life after death. The findings of archeologists all over the world fall into this same pattern. Here in Iowa the traces of prehistoric civilization are found in caves and along the rivers where primitive man made his home.

Many questions arise when we begin the study of the history of Iowa: How old is Iowa? What formed her fertile, rolling prairie lands? Who was the first man who made his home beside her flowing streams?

Chapter 1

UNKA—PREHISTORIC BOY
OF IOWA

Unka moved lazily on the floor of the dark cave. The dry marsh reeds crackled beneath him. He opened one eye.

He could hear his mother moving about in the outer cave. Unka opened his other eye and squinted toward the light.

This was the day! He sat up. Of course! This was the day! He threw his wolf pelt over his shoulder and fastened it with a sharpened bone.

"About time, Unka," Mother scolded. "Have you forgotten? We move up the Wide River* today." She stooped over the fire and turned the corn ears that were roasting in the coals.

"I almost forgot."

"Your father and brothers have been up since daylight. Already they are down by the Wide River."

Unka quickly scooped up an ear of the hot corn in a

---

* Mississippi River

shell and ran down the steep bank to the wide river, chewing on the hot corn greedily.

"Look! Sleepy One is up!" taunted Osah, Unka's older brother.

"We were about to leave you and go to the new land without you," teased Father. "While we would grow fat on our hunting, you would grow thin like the winter bear."

Unka knew they were only having fun with him. He climbed up in the lower branch of a tree and watched his brothers and father as they loaded the hollow-log canoe. Osah, the Hunter, carried his prized stone spear, mounted on the end of a straight hickory stick. He placed it carefully in the front of the canoe. Formo, the Fisher, Unka's other brother sat cross-legged on the bank sorting out his bone fish-hooks, while Father gathered up the stone hide scrapers, the hole piercers of fowl bone, and the new sling he had fashioned from a deer hide.

The move up the Wide River had long been Father's dream. "Someday I'm going to see what's beyond the Great Bow of the Wide River," Father had said.

Unka, too, had often thought about what lay beyond the Great Bow. The Wide River came flowing past Unka's cave from the land of the sunrise, then turned and flowed down toward the big rapids.

"There will be rich new valleys with many deer, forests full of berries and tender roots, and rivers alive with fish. I am sure there is a fine land beyond the Great Bow." For many moons Father could talk of nothing else.

"Run back to the cave," ordered Father. "Tell Mother to bring the last of the deer meat or we grow hungry on the Wide River."

Everyone was ordering him around this morning, Unka thought. When he reached the cave, it was Moth-

4

Maquoketa Caves in Jackson County

er again. "Look through the cave, Unka. See if I have left anything."

Unka crept into the inner cave, carrying a shell of flaming animal grease which Mother had thrust into his hand. He touched the cold walls. His fingers traced the drawings that adorned the walls. Unka was proud of the drawings, for Father had carved them with his sharpest stone ax—the Sun God, the Great Protector; the Thunderbird, who brought rain for the new corn, and the mammoth, that great-grandfather claimed to have seen in the olden days.

It would be strange living in a new cave.

"Come," called Father from the cave entrance. "It is time we go to the Sacred Grove and speak with our fathers."

With Father leading the way, Unka, Formo, and Osah walked through the tall grasses. Unka bounded about like a small deer. As they drew near to the cluster of trees rising from the open prairie, Father touched Unka with a warning hand. They were approaching sacred ground. Unka must be quiet, lest he disturb the sleeping fathers.

Father moved to the center of the grove. High above in the branches were the sleeping fathers. Father knelt in the drying grass. His expert hands worked the bow and drill to make a fire. A faint smell of burning grass floated across to Unka. When the spark jumped into flame, Unka and his brothers lay down at the grove's edge, burying their faces in the sweet smelling grass, as Father had taught them to do.

Father's voice rose above the wind, his hands outstretched to the sky, chanting the prayer to the gods who watched over Unka's ancestors. The chant went on and on. When would Father finish? Would the gods of the Sacred Grove allow them to leave the land, or would they show their displeasure and send the thunder rolling from the hills and the spear of lightning flashing across the sky?

The morning sun grew hot upon their backs. Finally Father stopped. He touched Unka, Osah, and Formo with the tip of his spear. It was over. With a loud cry Father ran through the grass toward the Wide River, waving his spear above his head.

"Surely the gods have given their blessings," shouted Osah, as he joined his father. Unka ran after them. He was happy. They would move up the Wide River. The Sun God had smiled on them.

The trip up the Wide River in the hollow-log canoe was strange and exciting.

The river often became angry. Swift rapids seized the boat and tumbled it from side to side, but Father was a skilled boatman. When the sun dropped behind the river bank, the family went ashore and slept beneath the sighing trees.

Through four sunrises and four sunsets the little group poled up river against the force of the Wide River.

"The water grows cold," Father shouted back from the front of the boat. "The Great Ice is near." He plunged the long pole deep into the water.

As they rounded a bend in the river, Unka saw a dazzling green expanse of light that almost blinded him.

"It is the Great Ice Sheet!" shouted Father.

Now Father stood up and guided the log boat toward the mass. As they approached the edge, Osah jumped into the water and pulled the craft up to the edge of the glacier. Before Unka could step out, Osah was shouting, "Look! Good Father! Beneath the ice!"

Unka scrambled out of the boat. A mass of woolly hair and two huge, curved ivory tusks protruded through the mass of ice.

"What is it?" screamed Unka.

"The ancient mammoth!" marveled Father.

"He is caught in the Ice Sheet," said Osah, stepping gingerly on the ice.

"How long has he been here?" asked Unka, retreating toward the boat, where Mother was holding the hollow-log against the river's pull.

"Many, many suns have opened their doors since this

"The ancient Mammoth!" marveled Father.

beast was alive," reassured Father. "The cold has kept
him this way."

"How big they were, Father! He must have stood as
tall as the sky!"

"Our ancient fathers have told tales of just such an
animal, but never did I think to see one. See his teeth."

"See the long hair. And underneath is woolly fur,"
added Osah, who was down on his hands and knees
looking closely at the mammoth.

"And a shaggy mane too," commented Formo.

"No man was safe when this ugly beast roamed the
land," said Father. "My father's father told of them."

"I would not have liked to have lived here then,"
Unka ventured, shaking his head.

But Father was no longer looking at the mammoth
caught beneath the ice. He was gazing at the ice sheet
stretching far into the horizon.

"It is true," he pondered, "what the wise ones told us. The ice sheet is surely melting." Father stooped and picked up a handful of wet soil at the glacier's edge. "See. The dirt is ground as fine as a woman's stone could grind it. But we better not stay here looking at this old fellow. We must go beyond the ice sheet if we want the Sun God to help us."

Father turned back to the Wide River. Formo and Osah followed. Unka stole one last glance at the huge mammoth and then ran to join his father.

The moon in the late summer sky changed from a round ball to a thin bow before the venturesome little family floated out upon a wide lagoon. The Wide River ceased its mad rush down stream. Far ahead stretched the Wide River, but toward the region of the rising sun wound another river.

"This is the place!" exclaimed Father, scanning the western shoreline, where lush green grasses crept up the high hills.

"Yes, Good Father," joined in Osah. "This is the place! See the herd of elk on the high peak?"

"And such fish!" chimed in Formo, peering over the side of the boat.

Father guided the boat ashore. Unka jumped from the canoe and clambered up the grassy bank. How good it was to feel the tall grasses against his legs! What a valley to explore! Osah disappeared with his spear up the highest hill. Formo was soon busy stalking along the water's edge with upraised harpoon.

Before Unka realized it, the sun was sinking beyond the high peak. Father's loud hallo echoed across the hills. Unka scampered back toward the Wide River.

Mother had not been idle while her sons were exploring the new land. She had found a cave far up the side of the river bank.

"It is high. It will be dry when the river runs full," she said proudly as she led the way to the new cave.

"It's bigger than our old cave," announced Unka.

He stood beside the cave entrance and looked out across the Wide River.

"See, Father. We have two rivers: the Wide River and the Small River. See how they join hands beyond the big lake."

"It is a fine home", agreed Father. "And above our cave I have found the high hill. It shall be the new home of our ancient fathers. We will move their bones from the Sacred Groves to our new land. My sons and I will build the mounds for them. We will shape the ground: an elk for Swift Foot, my father; a bear mound for Black One, my father's father. And for the ancient, ancient ones, which I knew not, the serpent."

The sun had disappeared behind the high hill. Mother started a fire in the mouth of the new cave. Formo came up from the Wide River carrying five big fish strung on a willow branch. He held up his catch. "Good harpoon!" he boasted.

But Osah, the Hunter, was not to be shamed by the exploits of his brother. He shouted from the top of the hill and came bounding down to the cave, a small deer slung across his shoulders.

"It is a good land," Father again reminded them. "And it is good to have sons who hunt the fish and the deer."

Osah threw the deer at his mother's feet. Mother began to skin the animal with a sharp stone held tightly in her strong hand.

"Now, Unka, bring the light," Father commanded.

"I must place the Sun God on the wall of our cave so that he will protect our new home." He strode into the cave. Unka picked up the shell of grease and knelt by the fire to light it, but before the flame could catch, Father's voice echoed from inside the cave.

"Run! Run! The Shaggy One!"

Father ran from the inner room of the cave. Behind him an enormous black bear lumbered from the darkness. A deep growl rumbled from the bear's throat. Osah, sensing the danger, jumped to the fire. He seized a flaming stick and rushed at the bear. The animal turned upon Osah. Osah waved the torch like a spear, thrusting it at the beast. With loud howls and shrieks, Osah drove the big bear ahead of him from the cave and down the river bank.

"He will never come back," laughed Father. "Once Black Bear has been burned out of his cave, he will not return." But to be sure that there were not other members of Black Bear's family living in the new cave, Father and Osah carried their flaming brands into the cave and poked into all the corners.

"You are a brave hunter, my son," said Father, patting the proud Osah on the back. "This was surely the anger of the Sun God. We have waited too long to place him on our cave wall. Bring the fire, Unka" He picked up his stone ax and returned to the inner cave. Sparks flew as Father's sharp stone chipped away in the rock. Unka held the light high. As the Sun God's head began to take form, Unka's head began to nod sleepily.

"The Little One is tired," laughed Osah. "Here, let me hold the light for Father."

Unka was glad to hand the sputtering grease to his brother and to creep over to the fire that was now brightly ablaze in the mouth of the cave. He pulled a rib bone

11

from the partially roasted deer meat that Mother had set over the fire. He lay down beside the blaze. The meat was good—juicy and brown.

The Moon God was peeping through the sky door just above the Wide River. Its light danced upon the moving water.

Unka snuggled down upon the dirt floor.

His new land! Beside the Wide River and the tall hill.

It was a beautiful land!

Chapter 2

THE LAY OF THE LAND

Iowa is a land of old and new, prairie and hill, farm and industry, corn and culture.

The squares and rectangles of the farm fields stretch 310 miles from the Mississippi River on the east to the Missouri and Big Sioux Rivers on the west and 200 miles from the state of Minnesota on the north to the state of Missouri on the south.

With the highest point, Ocheyedan Mound, in the northwest and the lowest point in Keokuk County, Iowa looks as if a prehistoric giant had picked up one corner and tipped it gently toward the southeast.

An almost unnoticeable divide extends from the Lake region in Dickinson County south to the Missouri state border. All streams west of the divide—such as the Floyd, Little Sioux, Boyer, Nishnabotna, and Nodaway—flow into the Missouri River. The Upper Iowa, Turkey, Maquoketa, Wapsipinicon, Cedar, Iowa, Skunk, and Des Moines flow east to the Mississippi River. These 900

The highest point in Iowa—Ocheyedan Mound

miles of inland streams make an excellent natural drainage system through Iowa's rich farm lands.

Ancient Iowa

Many elements worked together to make Iowa. The earth began perhaps five billion years ago. In some ancient age, often called the Palezoic Age, one-celled plant and animal life began to appear. At this time most of Iowa was under water. The shells and bones of sea life sank to the bottom of this inland sea and formed deposits of limestone.

Over the long expanses of time, the land began to rise from the sea. The climate became tropical. Jungle-like swamps covered Iowa. Huge ferns grew in the lush swamps, and salamanders and frog-like creatures moved about. This was the age of fishes. During a very gradual

14

rising and falling of the land, some of the rocks of Iowa, such as coal, were formed. Lead, zinc, and gypsum are found in these rocks.

Traces of the plant and animal life of this age have been found in the limestone quarries near Le Grand in Marshall County. Such traces are called fossils. Sea lilies with their long flexible necks and arms, starfish, and sea urchins appear as if carved into the stone. About forty different species of this prehistoric sea life have been found in Iowa. Fossilized starfish are very rare, yet one slab of Iowa limestone has 183 starfish on it.

Many millions of years later, Iowa became the home of dinosaurs and reptiles. This age is called the Middle or Mesozoic Age. Part of the time Iowa became a desert. Later the western part of Iowa slowly sank under the water again.

When Iowa had risen for the last time from the sea bottom, during the Modern or Cenozoic Age, the climate changed. Iowa became cold. Soon there was more snow and ice on the ground than would melt in the short summer.

The Glaciers

Four great glaciers came down from Canada and spread out southward over Iowa. The first glacier, the Nebraskan, covered all of Iowa. The second glacier, the Kansan, covered all of Iowa except a tiny corner in the northeast. The Illinoian glacier touched Iowa only in the southeastern part, but it pushed the Mississippi River nearly 50 miles westward. When this ice sheet melted, the Mississippi River returned to its original channel; such rivers as the Wapsipinicon, Cedar, and Maquoketa took its former glacial channel.

The last great glacier was known as the Wisconsin.

It came down in two tongues: one in north central Iowa; and when this melted, another tongue, called the Mankato, came down as far as Des Moines. This last glacier probably retreated not more than 11,000 years ago. Geologists estimate that each of the four glaciers lasted about 30,000 years.

The glaciers traveled very slowly carrying rocks and boulders from Canada and northern Minnesota which the glaciers ground up and scattered over the state. It is estimated that the glaciers traveled about one mile in ten years. As the glaciers moved, they scraped the land beneath smooth and deposited soil over the rocks. For many years the wind, rain, and frost worked upon the soil, blowing it about, washing it from the hillsides, and breaking it into fine particles. Plant life grew, died, and enriched the soil, giving Iowa a fertile layer of top soil that varies in depth from very thin in the eastern part of the state to many feet deep in the western part.

This gift of the soil from the glaciers has proven to be the wealth of Iowa, estimated to be equal in value to all the gold and silver mines in the world. 25% of all the grade-A land in the United States is found in Iowa.

What Iowa would have been like without these great ice sheets can be seen by visiting the northeast corner of the state. This area was covered by only the first glacier. Here are rocky cliffs and narrow gorges, hundreds of feet deep. In this section it is next to impossible to find a level stretch of land. This northeast part of the state, around Elkader, McGregor, Guttenberg, and Garnavillo, is usually referred to as the Little Switzerland of Iowa.

In the northwestern part of the state the glaciers left many lakes. Lake Okoboji and Spirit Lake make up the famous Lakes of Iowa. Iowa's Lake Okoboji is often referred to as one of the "blue water lakes" of the world.

Many elements worked together to make Iowa

The others are Lake Geneva in Switzerland and Lake Louise in Canada. Because of Okoboji's depth, over 250 feet in places, and its clear, spring-fed waters, it reflects Iowa's sky in such a way that the lake appears to be filled with blue water.

Climate

After the last glacier had melted, Iowa became a land of snowy winters, wet springs, and hot summers. This climate, coupled with the rich, well-drained soil, makes Iowa an ideal spot to grow corn, oats, soybeans, and hay.

About 150 days of the year are frost-free with the sun shining about 60% of the time. Temperatures vary from 25 degrees below zero in the winter to around 100 degrees in the summer. Iowa's average snowfall is about

17

30 inches in the winter, with the summer rainfall varying from an average of 26 inches in the north to 36 inches in the south. The early spring rains cause seed to sprout quickly; the hot summers with their frequent thunderstorms, hasten the growth, and the beautiful Indian summer days of autumn dry and mature the crop.

Because of these conditions, Iowa ranks first in the world in the production of corn. The value of one year's corn crop in Iowa has been estimated to be 30 times as much as was paid for the entire Louisiana Territory.

Industries Related to Climate and Soil

Much of Iowa's corn and grain is used in the raising of hogs, cattle, and poultry. The gently rolling hills and wooded bottom lands along the streams provide rich pasture land. The Iowa farmer at the beginning of the 20th century raised enough to feed himself and 26 others.

25% of all the grade A land in the United States is found in Iowa

Many industries in Iowa have grown up around agriculture. Meat packing plants prepare the hogs and cattle of Iowa for the markets of the world. Farm implement factories keep the farmer well supplied with modern tractors and farming equipment. Cereal mills process the corn and grain for breakfast tables. Tile and cement plants make use of the many deposits of sand and gravel that were left by the glaciers to provide drainage tile for the farms and modern roads and bridges for transportation.

At one time in Iowa's history, lead was mined, but the deposits were never plentiful enough to make this an important industry. Some coal deposits are found in southern Iowa, but the quality and the difficulty in mining this coal have kept this industry from being a profitable undertaking.

A Gypsum Giant

Today gypsum deposits provide the most important mining industry in Iowa. Iowa gypsum first came to the attention of the world through a hoax, the Cardiff Giant of the 1870's.

George Hull, a native of Connecticut, was visiting a sister in Ackley, Iowa, when he conceived the idea of "making" a prehistoric giant. He had found a 5-ton slab of gypsum near Fort Dodge. Perhaps as a practical joke or perhaps as a money-making scheme, Hull decided to carve the slab into the form of a giant, bury it, have it discovered, and declare that it was a petrified man.

With great difficulty, Hull had the slab of Iowa gypsum shipped forty miles by horse and wagon to a railroad station, and sent to a German stonecutter, Edward Burkhardt, in Chicago. Here, Hull, Burkhardt, and

19

two assistants carved the slab into the likeness of a man. They used mallets to puncture the surface of the gypsum so that it looked like human skin and bathed it in sulphuric acid to make it look old. The stone man was ten feet long, two and a half feet wide, and weighed 2,000 pounds when it was finished.

According to his plan, Hull had the giant crated and sent by rail to a relative, Stub Newell, a farmer near Cardiff, New York. Under Hull's direction, the giant was buried one night on the Newell farm, and a field of clover was planted over the spot to make the "discovery" look real.

A year later Newell decided to dig a well on his farm. He hired two men to dig the well over the place where he and Hull had buried the gypsum giant. The next day the citizens of Cardiff were amazed to learn that a petrified prehistoric giant had been found on the Newell farm.

Experts were called in. They declared that the stone man was certainly a petrified giant. The stone man was dubbed the Cardiff Giant. He immediately became world famous. He was displayed at fairs and circuses throughout the United States, and people paid money just to be able to look at him.

Eventually a Yale professor proved that the Cardiff Giant was no petrified man, but merely a carved piece of gypsum. The Giant was carted off and put into storage. He is now in the possession of the New York State Historical Association and can be seen today in the Farmers' Museum at Cooperstown, New York.

The Iowa gypsum deposits never again produced a Cardiff Giant, but they have given growth to a giant industry in Iowa. The gypsum plants of Fort Dodge are located over the heart of one of the purest and richest gypsum deposits in the world. The purity of the gypsum mined here averages 95%. This means that products made from Iowa gypsum are strong, uniform, and durable. Gypsum is used in the manufacture of wallboard, plaster, insulation, siding shingles, and weatherproof sheathing.

The glaciers, the weather, the soil—all worked together to prepare the geography of Iowa for the coming of man. History reveals how man took the land which he found between the rivers and molded it into the Hawkeye State as we know it today.

Chapter 3

THE FIRST IOWANS

As the last glacier was beginning to melt, a primitive hunter and his child roamed across the frigid edge of western Iowa looking for game. His only weapon was a flint-tipped spear. He knew of fire and its uses, but he had not yet discovered the bow and arrow.

He hunted bison larger than any alive today on the banks of the ancient Little Sioux River. He had learned that by taking a torch from his fire, he could drive the bison to their death over the steep cliffs. With his spear he could kill the crippled animals. He ate the meat of the bison which he roasted over his fire, sucking the marrow from the bones which remained.

This long-headed hunter wore skins of animals for clothes. He had no permanent home, but followed the game wherever it went. Since the bison came to the glacier's edge to drink, this ancient hunter often haunted these frozen wastelands. His life was cruel and hard, full of danger, hunger, and cold.

From Hunter to Farmer

We have learned that the climate and geography of the land underwent great changes in the early ages. Ancient man's greatest problem was food. If he could not find his food in one place, he could either move to another or he could change his way of living to fit his changing surroundings. As primitive man learned to change, he progressed.

Where did Iowa's ancient man come from?

To live, he had to hunt and kill animals that lived on the edge of the glaciers. Some think that in his search for food, he wandered from his frozen lands in Siberia and crossed into Alaska on a land bridge which once extended across the Bering Straits. This may have been as early as 20,000 B.C.

For thousands of years this *Paleo-Indian,* as archeologists have named him, lived by killing such game as the camel, the woolly elephant, and the giant bison. After the hunt he camped in small groups with his companions at the site of the kill. Sometime after the glacial ages, the Paleo-Indian devised a stone spear. This discovery made his hunting much easier.

The retreat of the glacial ice northward changed the plant and animal life, and many types of animals died out. The Paleo-Indian found that he must look elsewhere for his food.

Gradually the gathering of seeds was added to hunting as an important way to obtain food. By about 3,000 B.C., seed gathering probably became more important. This is indicated by the presence of seed-grinding tools. He found it more convenient to live in small camps with his fellow man, close to the places where such plant food could be found. These people are often referred to as *archaic gatherers.*

23

After approximately another 4,000 years, man added two more important discoveries to his culture: pottery and burial mounds. He still lived by hunting and gathering, but now he began to think of other things. He devised a type of religion to explain the mysteries of death. He built burial mounds up and down the Mississippi River Valley, where he buried his dead in elaborate ceremonies. He now lived in small villages and spent his time, when not searching for food, fashioning clay into crude dishes. He soon learned that if he did not take advantage of the food available in an area, other tribes would move in and use the supply. His life became one of hunting, gathering, fighting, and frequent migration. These men are often referred to as the *woodland mound builders.*

When the French came to explore Iowa, they found a group of Indians along the Mississippi River who were chiefly engaged in agriculture. They lived in large villages. They did a great amount of hunting, but they also relied upon their small garden plots for food. Some think these people may have been tribes who had moved up the Mississippi River from Mexico and mingled with the Indians along the upper Mississippi. The French explorers questioned these people about their history, but they knew little about their own past. These Indians thought that at one time they may have been a large, powerful nation, but they did not know for certain what had happened to their ancestors.

One can see, then, that the history of Iowa for thousands and thousands of years before the white man arrived was the story of the change and growth of man from hunter, seed gatherer, mound builder, to agriculturist.

The Turin Man

Since these prehistoric men left no written records of their age, one can only study their life from the remains that have been found: weapons, pottery, cave drawings, burial mounds, and bones. Iowa has long been a rich source of such information on prehistoric life.

One such archeological discovery came about when a dragline operator was hard at work one summer day in 1955, digging gravel from his pit near the little Monona County town of Turin in western Iowa. As he removed the earth from the steep bluff just a block from the little town's main street, he noticed that the bucket of his dragline had uncovered a pile of bones and a human skull.

Asa Johnston was not sure what he had found. He hurriedly called a coroner. The two men dug out a portion of the skeleton with a hand shovel, but when they tried to lift it, the bones crumbled into dust. Archeologists were called in to examine the remainder of the bones. Careful examination and radioactive carbon tests determined that the man was a 30-year old man who had lived in Iowa around 2700 B.C. Because the discovery was found near Turin, they called him the Turin Man.

Twenty feet beyond the Turin Man, a gopher had dug his tunnel down into the bluff, weakening the hillside. As the archeologists dug carefully into the gravel, about a ton of loosened gravel caved in around them. Three of the scientists were nearly buried, but when they dusted themselves off, there was another skeleton, that of a child.

The scientists took two days to remove these bones. They first covered them with plaster-soaked burlap strips. When this hardened they lifted the bones and dirt in the plaster jacket and removed them to the Sanford Museum at Cherokee, where they can be seen today.

The Turin gravel pit proved to be a "history book" on the life of Iowa's earliest citizens. Two more skeletons were found, an adolescent and a baby. At the feet of the adolescent was a spear point. Around the neck of the other was a string of snail shell beads. The teeth of the Turin Man and his family were good, but showed signs of being worn down. No doubt these ancient people had feasted on bison, for many bison bones were scattered nearby.

Later, near the small Cherokee County town of Quimby, searchers found a pile of bison bones heaped around the charcoal of an ancient fire. Stone knives and skin scrapers found nearby showed that the early hunters had butchered the animals at the site and roasted them over their fire.

Surely the Turin Man and his family were some of Iowa's earliest inhabitants.

The Lewis-Hill Survey

Iowa has thousands of burial mounds scattered throughout the state, but often farmers have plowed over the mounds and earthworks left by early man, destroying their location. Much information is available today because two men set out over 70 years ago to map and preserve the ancient cave drawings of the Mississippi River bluffs, the mounds of northeast Iowa, and the earthworks which were scattered over the prairies. What these men found provides another page in the history book of Iowa's earliest citizens.

The flickering lantern cast weird shadows that danced along the cave wall. With one hand holding the oiled paper against the cave wall, Theodore Lewis traced with care. As his pencil rubbed over the indentations, a picture began to form.

"Ummm. Looks like the Sun God again," he mused as he blacked in the lines.

The sound of horse hoofs clambering up the steep trail to the cave caused him to turn from his work.

"That you, Ned?" he called out from the dark cave.

"That she be," came the reassuringly familiar voice.

Lewis took the paper down from the wall, scrawled "Allamakee County" in the corner, and placed it upon a stack of similar drawings.

The rider stepped into the cave, blinking in the dimness.

"Got some ready for me today?" he inquired.

Lewis pointed to the pile of drawings on the cave floor. "All of those. Wait, and I'll wrap them."

He went to his gear and took out an oilskin sheet. Patiently he rolled the drawings into a scroll and tied them firmly with a cord, tucking the ends of the oilskin around the edges.

"Are you starting down river right away?" asked Lewis.

"Might as well. As long as the weather holds," the rider answered. "I should be able to make McGregor by night."

"Bring me some more paper this trip. There's more drawings in these caves than I ever dared hope to find."

The pictures which Lewis was tracing were made by some ancient Iowan to decorate the walls of his cave home. The ancient man had grooved the rock with a stone hammer, making outlined pictures of the Sun God, figures of men and women, and animals such as the mammoth, bison, turtle, and beaver. Often the figure that emerged on Lewis' paper was that of a man dressed

27

in the costume of the Sun God or sometimes a man in an elaborate headdress. Surely the cave drawings were as old as the mammoth, and mammoths roamed Iowa around 8,000 B.C.

Theodore Lewis, a robust young surveyor from Richmond, Virginia, came to St. Paul, Minnesota, while still in his 20's. The sturdy, sun-burned surveyor caught the attention of Alfred J. Hill, a successful businessman. As a hobby, Hill had begun to make drawings of prehistoric Indian mounds around St. Paul. He knew the land west of the Mississippi was rich in such mounds. He had often stopped off along the Iowa bluffs that lined the river. If only he could find some young man who would go out and survey the mounds, he could make the drawings, for he was an excellent draftsman. When he saw the strong young surveyor, Lewis, he knew he had found his man.

Hill invited Lewis to his home in St. Paul and excitedly explained his plan. "You will work in the field: Minnesota, Iowa Wisconsin. . .wherever you can find this type of mounds. Here's the way we'll do it. You survey every mound, make exact measurements, and send your findings to me. I will make up the maps from your figures.. I'll pay you $3 a day for every day you work."

Young Lewis agreed to the terms.

Lewis-Hill Survey was started in 1881. It was hard work for the young surveyor, starting in the spring of each year and stopping only when the cold Iowa winters forced him inside.

Lewis could never forget the day he first landed in northeast Iowa from the river steamer. He walked up from the wharf through the little town of McGregor with his engineer's level slung across his back and his leather bound notebooks bulging from the pouch at his side.

"Any Indian mounds around here?" Lewis asked. An old fellow squinted off into the bluffs. "Whole bunches of them up there."

"Any Indian mounds around here?" he asked.

An old fellow, lounging on main street, squinted off into the bluffs, "Whole bunches of them up there."

And what a wealth of mounds he had found! No wonder these mounds had escaped the farmer's plow and the tourist's curiosity. They were situated on top of a high hill. The trail wound up around the hillside like a mountain path. And the mounds were effigy mounds. This meant that each mound was made in the pattern of some figure, always in profile. If the effigy represented a man or animal, it was always shown lying down on its right side with the nose pointing downstream. Even the bird and snake mounds suggested by their wings or head that they were moving toward the water.

Lewis often wondered what strange idea had compelled this ancient man to carry and handle yards and yards of earth just to bury some bones.

The Effigy Mounds of McGregor

At the McGregor site, Lewis surveyed 6 mounds that stretched out in a straight line, 3 bear, 2 bird, 1 oval, and 82 shaped like a cone. One bird mound had a wing spread of 171 feet. Altogether there were 94 mounds in this group. From Dubuque on up into Minnesota for a stretch of 100 miles, Lewis surveyed and measured a line of mounds and ancient earthworks that was almost continuous. In the group there was a woman mound with arms upraised, 70 ft. by 145 ft. Most of the mounds were from three to five feet high, with the largest mound extending over 300 feet in length. One group of mounds consisted of ten bears strung out in marching formation.

Some of the mounds were not burial sites but appeared to be an earth wall that may have served as the foundation for a fortress. Lewis had read that it was thought the ancient man had built a crude type of shelter on the low mounds. When the owner of the hut died, his family buried him under the center of the home and then burned it down. That was probably why Lewis often found pottery, flint and stone weapons, and rude ornaments in the mound. Perhaps the mounds were also used to send smoke signals to neighboring tribes.

These woodland mound builders, according to recent soil tests, probably lived in Iowa from the time of Christ up to the time of the Crusades, about 1200 A.D. Perhaps, as some historians believe, they were ancestors of the historic woodland and plains Indians of the Mississippi

River Valley. From studies made of their ancient camps, men have determined that they raised beans, tobacco, squash, melons, and corn. They were probably skillful boatmen, and, no doubt, they told stories of their heroes and wove legends of the mythical powers of their gods. Something in the creative mind of this primitive mound builder made him feel it necessary to leave his record on the walls of his cave dwelling and in the mounds of his dead.

The Lewis-Hill archeological survey cost $16,200. The bill was paid by Hill, but the miles were covered by Lewis: 10,000 miles of foot travel plus 10,000 miles of travel by rail, steamer and horse during the fifteen years. The headquarters for the survey was Hill's house in St. Paul. It took one whole room to store the data on the 13,087 mounds that he had surveyed and the 100 large paper sheets of the original, full-sized rubbings of the rock carvings from the Mississippi River caves.

When the survey ended with Hill's death in 1895, 1,000 sheets of neatly drawn mound groups, earthworks, and cave drawings had been assembled by the two men. Today the Lewis-Hill material, owned by the Historical Society of Minnesota, is an important source of information on the life of Iowa's earliest citizens.

1,204 acres of the Effigy Mound area which Theodore Lewis surveyed near McGregor was set aside in 1949 as a National Monument, the only National Monument in Iowa. Visitors can climb the winding trails to the tall bluff and see the outlined figures as left by these primitive mound builders.

With the Explorers

With the Explorers (1673-1805)

The French were the first to bring to Iowa's history the daring adventures of the white man. While Britain was struggling to get colonies started along the Atlantic seacoast, France had a different idea as to the best way to gain control of the New World. The French plan was to spread colonies out along the great waterways: The St. Lawrence River, the Great Lakes, and the Mississippi River.

Control of the waterways meant control of the fur trade. France believed this to be the great wealth of the new continent. In 1673, Marquette and Joliet were sent by the Governor of New France to explore the Mississippi and to claim for France all the land on either side. They explored as far as the Arkansas River. LaSalle completed the trip to the Gulf of Mexico in 1682. He named the entire region *Louisiana* in honor of the King of France and claimed for France all of the land drained by the Mississippi and its tributaries.

Iowa remained a part of France until the end of the French and Indian War. This struggle for power between Britian and France ended in 1763 with the British getting all of the land east of the Mississippi River.

Because Spain had aided France in the war, France gave to Spain the land west of the Mississippi. Iowa then became a part of Spain. At the time Dubuque took possession of the lead mines at Catfish Creek, he received a title to the mines from the Spanish governor at St. Louis.

When Napoleon rose to power in France in the early 19th century, the Spanish were persuaded to return Louisiana to France. Iowa again became a part of France.

Napoleon had plans for restoring to France its lost empire in the New World. His plans changed for several reasons. The outbreak of yellow fever among his troops on Santo Domingo Island made him realize the island could not be used as a French naval base to protect the New World Empire. Without the base, he feared the power of the mighty British fleet. He also needed money to continue his conquest of the Eureopean continent. When the American offer came to buy New Orleans, he offered the sale of all of Louisiana for fifteen million dollars.

The purchase was made in 1803, when Thomas Jefferson was President. Iowa, for the first time, became a part of the United States. From then on, American explorers—Lewis and Clark on the west and Pike on the east— moved into the new land, sending back reports of the wealth and vastness of the new land bargain.

This unit will show that Iowa was touched by the Old World as France tried to get control of the interior of the continent. Trade was established between the Indians and the French. A mining industry was set up by Dubuque and trade between Dubuque's settlement and St. Louis was started. The explorations by the American government after the Louisiana Purchase paved the way for further settlement.

Chapter 4

BLACKGOWN EXPLORER
—MARQUETTE

Jaques Marquette was born and grew up in the shadow of the Church. He felt the pull of the Church very early in his life. His mother encouraged him to make this his life's work.

Marquette's family in France had distinguished itself as a family of soldiers and statesmen. His father, proud of this tradition, was disappointed when he discovered that his son was thinking of entering the service of the Church. It was a hard decision for young Marquette to make—to give up the tradition of his family.

Marquette's father, perhaps, would not have given in to his son's wishes if he had realized what the boy really had in mind, for young Marquette's thoughts were not about becoming a parish priest in France. Nor, with the influence of the family name, was he thinking about becoming a bishop or even filling a higher office in the

Church. His desire was to become a Jesuit priest and to take Christianity to the Indians in the New World.

Jesuits had been going along with the French trappers and traders ever since the French explorations had begun. In addition to taking Christianity to the Indians, priests were well educated men who could help make the maps and keep the records. Marquette wanted to become a missionary when his studies were completed in France.

Marquette Meets Joliet

The period of preparation for a Jesuit missionary was a long one. Sometimes Marquette grew impatient with the long years of study. He was twenty-nine years old when his years in school were finally over. His orders came to report in Quebec for missionary duty. He reached Quebec in September of 1666. He was told to stay there until his new orders came to go to a mission.

Marquette was lonely in Quebec. He was away from his family, his friends, and his country. He even felt at times as though he had lost contact with his Church. The old familiar churches and cathedrals were not to be found in this raw new country. It made him feel cut off from his faith.

It may have been that he met Joliet one evening as he went out walking to ease the pangs of loneliness. His eye caught the figure of a young man walking ahead of him. The energy he possessed was evident in his purposeful stride, in the bouyancy of his step, in the swing of his arms.

Suddenly the young man stopped, turned, and looked at the black-gowned priest. He waited until Marquette came up to him.

"I could feel you behind me," the young man said.

"Something compelled me to stop. Are you a newcomer to Quebec?"

Marquette fell in step with the young man and found himself telling the story of his background, his family, his dreams, and his purpose in life. Suddenly he realized he knew nothing about his companion, not even his name.

"My desire for company seems to have made me discourteous," Marquette said. "I haven't even asked your name."

The young man laughed.

"That is quite all right," he said. "I'll take my turn at talking now. My name is Louis Joliet. I was born here in Quebec. My story is quite different. You come from a wealthy family. My father was a poor wagonmaker. I can't even remember him. He died when I was very young. My mother had all she could manage to keep her family together, but we survived. As a matter of fact, we thrived on poverty. Most people in this country do, you know. Besides poverty, the winters are long and cold here. We live in constant dread of an Indian attack, but we have learned to laugh. You either laugh in the face of calamity, Father, or else you don't survive."

Marquette liked this young man. His intelligence was obvious, and his range of interests was wide. His conversation included music, philosophy, map-making. Marquette became curious as to just what this remarkable young man did for a living.

"Tell me, Joliet, are you a teacher?" Marquette said.

"No," answered Joliet, "I am not a teacher, although I am flattered that you might think me so. I haven't really made up my mind as to what I am. Four years ago I decided to become what you are—a Jesuit priest. Then I began to study music and philosophy. I have been given a chance to go to France for more study. I'm trying to make up my mind as to what I should do. I'm not sure what I want."

"The needs of the Church are great," said Marquette, "but the call of the Church should be very clear."

"I know there is no doubt within you, Marquette, that you have been called by the Church, but with me it is different. Perhaps a year in France will help me make up my mind."

The chance meeting of these two men had turned into a real friendship by the time Marquette was called to his mission and Joliet left for France. They had no way of knowing that Fate would throw them together again.

Marquette Among The Indians

Marquette was sent to work among the Indians at the trading station of Three Rivers. Located seventy-seven miles above Quebec, it was in the heart of the wilds. Father Gabriel Druilletes, who was at the mission, was a kind and patient teacher.

The lessons that had to be learned were difficult ones. How to live on little food while enduring the cold and wet of the wilds, the trick of handling a canoe in an icy current, the way to gain the friendship of the Indians were all a part of the training program a successful missionary must go through. But Marquette's desire to succeed overcame the frailness of his body. His ability to learn quickly made it possible for him to master six Indian dialects.

"Well, Marquette, you are an apt pupil," Gabriel said to him one day. "You have been with me now for a little more than a year. I think the time has come for you to have a mission of your own."

His chance had finally come! Fear, excitement, and elation were all mixed up inside of him. He was not strong, he knew, but surely desire was more important than strength. With God's help he knew he could not fail.

He was sent to Sault St. Marie in the summer of 1668. A year later he was given charge of a mission at La Pointe, a desolate spot on the southern shore of Lake Superior. This was the opportunity for which he had been waiting.

Marquette had actually just gotten started with his mission work among the Huron Indians when they were attacked by the Sioux. They fled to Mackinac Island. Marquette went with them and set up a new mission. It became known as the Mission of St. Ignace. It was a small mission and very poor. If Marquette sometimes felt lonely in his chosen work, he also felt that he was carrying out a high purpose in life by bringing Christianity to the Indians. This brought him comfort.

An Old Friend Returns

A year passed. One day in December of 1672, a boat arrived from Quebec. Marquette paused outside his door to watch the boat being unloaded. Something about the vigorous movements of one of the boatmen caught his eye. The man reminded him of his friend, Joliet, whom he had met six years before. He knew it could not be Joliet, for he was in France. Just then the man turned, saw Marquette, and flung up his hand in greeting.

"Hello, my friend! Why aren't you down at the bank to greet me?"

It was Joliet!

"What are you doing here? I thought you were in France."

39

Joliet laughed as he continued with an unbroken rhythm to unload the boat.

"I stayed in France only a year, then I came back to Quebec to become an explorer."

"An explorer!" exclaimed Marquette. "What a dangerous and exciting life you must have had!"

"I've learned many things since I saw you last," Joliet continued. "I've learned to find my way through the forests, to make canoes and weapons, to live with the Indians, and to survive on almost nothing."

"And now you are through with this exploring? Is that why you have come to see me?" asked Marquette.

"On the contrary. I am only beginning," answered Joliet. "The biggest exploration of all is now to be made. You know the great mystery—of the Great River? And where it flows? The Governor of New France* wants this mystery cleared up, and he has entrusted this most important project to us."

"Did you say 'to us'?" Marquette asked uncertainly. "Did you mean to include me?"

"Of course," Joliet turned quickly and looked directly at the slender, black-gowned man. "The orders are here in my pocket."

With one sweep of his arm he gaily embraced his friend as he handed him the instructions from the Governor. "Come, let us go and start making our plans."

Preparation for the Journey

All through that winter the two worked, carefully constructing their two boats of birchbark. They used spruce for the ribs. The boats had to be strong, for they knew the current of the Great River would be swift.

40

* Name denoting French holdings in America.

The boats must be light too. They would have to be carried over portages.[1]

The maps had been carefully drawn from whatever information was available on the Great River and were tighly rolled, waiting to point the way. The food had been carefully selected. Smoked meat and corn packed easily and kept better than most food.

Now all the preparations were made. Waiting for the weather to break was the only thing left to do.

"Tell me, Marquette, are you sure you are strong enough to go on this trip?" Joliet asked his companion as they sat before the fire one evening.

"Well, Joliet, my spirit of adventure is as great as yours," replied the priest. "Who does not want to solve the mystery of the Great River?"

"But you, my friend, are not an explorer," answered Joliet.

"Perhaps not an explorer," said Marquette. "And yet, you, my French brother, know this trip will give me an opportunity to spread Christianity to more people."

He reached forward and stirred the dying embers thoughtfully.

"Yes, Joliet, you expose yourself for the discovery of new lands. I expose myself to bring salvation to new people. I think perhaps we are both explorers."

The Explorers Begin Their Adventure

The morning of the seventh of May, 1673, dawned clear and bright. The ice had left the straits. There was warmth in the sun. The time had come for the journey.

Five Frenchmen who were fearless, experienced boatmen had been chosen to go with them. Swiftly they

---

[1] A portage is a carrying of boats and supplies overland between streams.

The Mississippi River from the McGregor Heights

packed the provisions. They took their places in the two canoes, the rangers and Joliet dressed in buckskin with their weapons beside them and Marquette in the long black gown of a Jesuit.

The group crossed Lake Michigan, entered Green Bay, and went up the Fox River. They portaged a mile and a half to the Wisconsin River and launched their canoes. As the current carried them downstream, no one knew where it would take them. Only time would tell.

The First Glimpse of Iowa Land

A month had passed since they had left the mission at St. Ignace. On the morning of June seventeenth, they noticed the navigation of the Wisconsin River becoming more difficult. As the current grew stronger, the canoes began to go faster. They swept out onto a huge river with the shores a mile apart. Everyone knew they had reached the Mississippi. They were at the foot of a high cliff. To the west were the wooded hills and beautiful prairies of what is now Iowa.

There can be no doubt that Marquette and Joliet felt the inspiration of their great discovery. Here before them was this magnificent river and all around them was this beautiful region, completely silent. Nowhere was there a sign of another human being.

They proceeded down the river, cautiously at first. They stopped from time to time to make camp, to catch fish, to explore the land, but always there was silence. And always there was the boundless prairie, scattered with herds of buffalo and elk. Down, down the river they made their way. One day cities would spring up on those beautiful shores, but now there was nothing but silence.

On and on they paddled their canoes. One day, another day, and still another, and nothing broke the stillness but the call of the birds as they circled in the air, the whisper of the wind as it blew through the trees, the thump of the fish as they hit the bottom of the boats. For eight days they went down the river.

A Footprint on the Shore

On the twenty-fifth day of June the spell was broken. As they beached their canoes and made preparation for camp, they made a discovery.

"Marquette! Come quickly!" Joliet was bent over examining the ground. "Look! A human footprint!" he exclaimed, as the priest hurried to his side. "And see! A path beyond that goes up to the bluff. Shall we follow it?"

There was no hesitation as Marquette answered, "By

Marquette and Joilet discover human footprints on Iowa soil.

all means. Let us go quickly and see where the path leads."

They followed the trail westward and discovered an Indian village on the banks of what was probably the Iowa River. They could see two other villages on a distant hill. They were close enough to see Indians moving about in the village. They approached until they were close enough to hear the Indians talking. They had not been seen. Marquette and Joliet looked at each other. Fear and uncertainty showed on both their faces. Should they reveal themselves? What if the Indians were hostile?

With prayers in their hearts, they both shouted in unison.

Quickly the Indians turned and saw the white men. There seemed to be a dispute among them as to which of them should come. Then four old men slowly walked toward them making signs of friendship and offering the peace pipe.

Marquette and Joliet were relieved when they saw this ceremony of the peace pipe that was performed only among friends.

Marquette spoke to them, "What tribe are you?"

"Illinois," they told him and offered their pipes to smoke. "We welcome you to our village."

The Indians courteously took them to the chief. When they came to him, the chief said, "How beautiful the sun is when you come to visit us. All our village awaits you."

They smoked the peace pipe while a feast was being prepared in their honor. The food that was served consisted of corn meal seasoned with oil, fish, roast dog, and roast buffalo. When the roast dog was offered to them, Marquette and Joliet looked at each other. They both knew that even at the price of peace they could not eat roast dog. The Indians, however, were not offended. They politely removed the dog meat when their guests declined.

Marquette and Joliet were delighted with the friendly reception they had received. They were equally delighted with the bountifulness of this land and with the

45

beauty of the prairie. This was Iowa and the people of Iowa as the white man first saw them.

They stayed with their Indian friends for six days. The friendship and the feeling of brotherhood grew as Marquette told them that he had been sent to them to bring them the Christian message. Marquette and Joliet told them they must soon go on and complete the exploration of the Great River.

As the explorers prepared to leave, the chief said to them, "I thank the Blackgown and his friend for coming to visit us. Never has the earth been so beautiful or the sun so bright as today. Never has the river been so calm or so free of rocks, never our tobacco so good or our corn so fine."

As a parting gift, the chief gave the explorers a little Indian boy for a slave.

The Indians did not want their new friends to go any farther south on the river. They were afraid they would find Indians who would not be friendly. They gave them a peace pipe to take with them to help secure safe passage.

The Explorers Turn Back

Marquette and Joliet left the friendly Indians of Iowa and went on farther south. They went past the mouth of the Illinois River, the Missouri River, and finally the Arkansas River.

"The river keeps going south," Joliet said to his companion. "I don't think there is much chance that it goes to the Gulf of California."

"It must go to the Gulf of Mexico," Marquette concluded. "We will not only be running into some hostile Indians, but if we go much farther south we will be seeing some hostile Spaniards."

"That would seem to be true," agreed Joliet. "For our own safety we had better turn back."

The trip home was begun on July seventeenth. The heat and mosquitoes became unbearable. Their strength began to leave them as they paddled upstream. Marquette began to show signs of the strain. At times he was near the point of collapsing.

Fortunately for them some friendly Illinois Indians told them a shorter way to return. They went up the Illinois River and the Chicago River and reached Lake Michigan. There Marquette and Joliet parted company.

The Death of Marquette

At the end of the four months' trip, Marquette was ill and exhausted. He remained at Green Bay to rest. The following year he returned to Illinois to visit the Indians, but again he became ill. He prayed for a return of health, but he grew steadily worse. He tried to get back to his mission at St. Ignace. Two of his faithful Indian friends tried to make it back by canoe with Marquette in the bottom of the boat, but his frail body could not stand the trip. He died before they could reach the mission. He was thirty-eight years old.

Marquette was never fitted for the rough life, but he seemed to have a strength and a faith that sustained him. He brought to the Indians of Iowa the idea that the white man could be gentle and loving and kind.

Joliet Returns to Quebec

Joliet had left Marquette to go back to Quebec. He had carefully written his report to the Governor of New France, made his maps, and completed his journal. After having traveled over 2500 miles, he got caught in the LaChine Rapids in the St. Lawrence River as he ap-

The Marquette-Prairie du Chien Bridge

proached Montreal. His canoe was overturned. All of his carefully prepared records were lost. His French boatmen and the little Indian slave drowned. Joliet was pulled out of the river by some fishermen and saved.

Joliet lived a long time after that, exploring around Hudson Bay. He died sometime around 1700; no one knows the exact day.

Marquette and Joliet, the first white men to come to Iowa, were met with a warm welcome and tokens of friendship. Between the Indians and the white men there was a feeling of kindness and respect. The wars and bad feeling were to come later.

Present day reminders of this journey of long ago are the markers at the mouth of the Wisconsin River as it enters the Mississippi at the town of McGregor, the town of Marquette close by, and the Marquette-Prairie du Chien Bridge that spans the Mississippi at this point.

Chapter 5

DUBUQUE STOPS THE SUN

The boy sat quietly, listening. Excitement was growing inside of him. The French traders were returning to the village on the banks of the St. Lawrence River. The boy had been waiting all week for their return. Now he heard the unmistakable sounds, the rhythmic paddling of the birch canoes and the coarse shouting voices of the men.

He had grown up hearing the sounds of traders leaving and traders coming home. Sometimes missionaries went with them. More often they went alone. The fur trade with the Indians took the traders first to the Great Lakes, then down the Wisconsin River. Now they were returning from the Mississippi River, where the Sac and Fox Indians had their villages.

He had grown up hearing stories about the Indians. The most exciting stories were about the Sac and Fox. How brave and cunning they were! He felt a stir of impatience as he waited for the traders to beach their canoes and unload their furs. Then the stories would be told. The best stories would be about the Indians.

The boy, Julien Dubuque, knew what he was going to do when he became a man. He would take his own canoe and he would go trade with the Indians. Perhaps if he were lucky, he could go live with them.

Arrival at Prairie du Chien

It was June in 1785. Julien Dubuque's dream had come true. He was now a young man guiding his birch canoe over the waters of the Mississippi. He had brought with him blankets, trinkets, beads, and other such things he knew the Indians liked. With a sure, steady stroke of the paddle, he approached the trading post at Prairie du Chien.

Getting established as a trader at Prairie du Chien was quite easy. The Sac and Fox liked this gay young Frenchman. He was different from the other traders who had come from the Far North country. He was different from the missionaries too. He took time to play with the Indian children. He talked to the busy Indian women. He listened to the braves as they told their stories of hunt and of war.

The Indians had a name for him. Dubuque was of small size. Because he was a French Canadian, he had dark skin. They called him "Little Night".

Dubuque soon found out that he could profit from being friendly with the Indians. They had furs to trade, and they wanted the presents he could give them. Sometimes he could get many furs for a few blankets, some shot, and cheap trinkets.

This black-haired French Canadian might have continued trading for furs if he had not heard rumors about the Indians digging for lead. He listened to the stories

An old lead shot tower still stands at Dubuque

carefully. He decided the lead mines were across the
Mississippi River. A tribe of Fox had their village on
Catfish Creek. He would go there.

The Lead Mines at Kettle Chief's Village

Quickly Dubuque packed his canoe with blankets
and trinkets. He found Kettle Chief's village at the
mouth of Catfish Creek. His quick eye saw the pretty
Indian maiden, Potosa, watching him as he gave presents
to the chief.

"Perhaps," thought Dubuque, "Potosa will tell me
where the lead mines are."

He saw Potosa coming toward him.

Dubuque held some beads on the tip of his fingers, swaying them gently back and forth. Potosa's eyes caught the glint of the beads in the sunlight.

"Would you like to have these beads, Potosa?" he asked.

"They are very pretty." Her voice betrayed her desire.

"You may have them," said Dubuque. "Will you tell me where the braves find the lead in the ground?"

The beads glittered.

Potosa reached out to take the beads from his hands. "Go behind Kettle Chief's village. Go back into the hills. There Little Night will find the lead."

Potosa left, the promised beads held tightly in her hands.

The secret of the lead mines was his! Dubuque quivered with excitment at the thought. He knew what he must do. A treaty must be signed with the Fox braves.

Dubuque spent much of his time learning the habits and customs of the Indians. As time passed, Kettle Chief and the braves became his good friends.

Adopted into the Tribe

One evening Dubuque saw the braves getting ready for a ceremonial dance. He sat at the edge of the circle watching the firelight on their faces as the Indians put on their headdress. Kettle Chief approached Dubuque, took his hand, and led him to the inner circle around the fire.

"I cannot do your dance," he said, pulling back.

"You need not do the dance," said the Chief. "We will make you, Little Night, our brother. You are the

52

first white man to live on this side of the river. We will make you a part of the tribe."

A great honor had come to him, Dubuque knew.

The Signing of the Treaty

After Dubuque had been adopted into the tribe, he signed a treaty with the Fox braves.

"What do you braves want the treaty to say?" he asked them.

"Little Night may have the mines as long as he wants," they answered him. "No Indian will work the mines nor any other white man."

Dubuque drew up the contract and explained to them what the paper said. Kettle Chief and the braves put their mark on the piece of paper. The mines and all the land around them were now his.

Excited and happy over the treaty, Dubuque climbed to the top of the bluff and looked around. Off to the south, the great river wound itself in and out among the islands and out of sight. Behind him the wooded hills unrolled, showing the first hint of the blaze of color that fall would bring.

Slowly he walked down the bluff to the village. Plans for a settlement near the lead mines were now forming in his mind.

He got ten white men from Prairie du Chien to clear the land and build the cabins. They built a mill and a furnace to smelt the ore.

One day he approached Kettle Chief with an offer.

"How many braves can Kettle Chief spare to work in the mines for Little Night?" asked Dubuque.

For the first time since Dubuque had been living with them, the Indian chief showed signs of great displeasure.

53

The city of Dubuque as it looks today.

"How did I offend the Great Kettle Chief?" asked Dubuque.

"Braves do not work in the mines!" exclaimed Kettle Chief. "The women will do the work."

Tunnels were made into the side of the hills. The Indian women carried the ore out in baskets and took it to the smelting furnace. Sometimes the old Indian men would carry some of the baskets. Dubuque was glad Kettle Chief had told him not to ask the braves. He could keep their friendship better if they did not know this.

Dubuque Uses Trickery

Many stories are told how Dubuque tricked the Indians into thinking he had magical powers. One story is that he claimed to be able to handle poisonous snakes

54

without their biting him. Once when he thought they were going to disobey him, he picked up a poisonous snake. The Indians watched, terrified. The snake crawled up his arm. Kettle Chief and the braves rushed forward. Potosa forgot her place was to stay with the Indian women and she, too, pushed forward.

"Little Night!" they cried, "The snake will kill you!"

Dubuque draped the snake around his shoulders.

"The snake will not hurt me," he said, "but you must listen to what I say."

Now the time had come to resort to his so-called magic again. He was working the Indians too hard, Dubuque knew, but he had to get a load of ore down the river to St. Louis. Twice a year he had been sending two or three boatloads of ore and furs. The ore found a ready market in the bustling St. Louis settlement, for the lead mines in Iowaland had been a source of ore for lead shot even during the Revolutionary War. It was almost time for the boats to be sent to St. Louis again. But there were not enough furs and ore to fill the boats. He had to do something to get the Indians to work harder.

The story is told that he called the white men to him and told them to go up the creek and pour oil on the water. Then he summoned the Indians together.

"The boats must go down the Father of Waters by the end of the week," he announced, "or the Great Water will burn up. I will make Catfish Creek burn up now!"

Dubuque stepped to the stream and set fire to it. The Indians did not know the men had poured oil on the water upstream. Terrified at the thought of the river being burned up, they hurried to do the work Dubuque asked.

Another tale sometimes told about Dubuque concerns his making use of an eclipse. According to the story, when Dubuque knew there was to be an eclipse of the sun, he asked Kettle Chief to assemble the entire village. They sat in a circle on the ground. Dubuque stepped to the center.

"Listen, all Kettle Chief people," he said. "Little Night has shown you much magic in the past. He will now show you even greater magic. The sun will grow dark in the sky!"

The sky was already beginning to darken. Dubuque's voice came like a roar of thunder.

"Oh, Sun!" he cried. "Hear Little Night. Hide your face in the sky!"

Darkness settled across the land.

The Indians sat motionless. This white man who had come to live with them was surely a god!.

Dubuque motioned for them to leave. Quietly they slipped away to their lodges. There was much to think about. They would never again doubt Little Night's power.

The boats were loaded by the end of the week.

Getting Title to the Mines of Spain

The title to the mines had begun to worry Dubuque. That was one reason why he had to get the boats on their way to St. Louis. He had to see the Spanish governor there and have him grant him the land where the lead mines were located.

The land on the west side of the Mississippi belonged to Spain. Dubuque knew that. He knew that France had given it to Spain at the end of the French and Indian War. This had not bothered him at first. He had thought only about a treaty with the Indians. He knew now that this was not enough. The title to the mines must be granted him by the Spanish governor.

When Dubuque went to St. Louis twice a year, it was always an event. The people in St. Louis liked him just as the Indians did. He had polite French manners. He was a gay and charming guest at the balls given in his honor. His arrival in St. Louis always created a stir. The Fox braves he took with him added to the picture of a wealthy trader from a wild country. The Mississippi was the dividing line between civilization and the wilds. Dubuque and his men were the only white people living west of the river. This made him seem even more daring and adventuresome.

When he arrived in St. Louis this time, he was granted an audience with the governor.

Dubuque bowed low as he entered the governor's office. "I am indeed grateful that you took the time to see this humble servant," said Dubuque. "I have signed a treaty with the Sac and Fox for the lead mines at Catfish Creek. But I know the land belongs to the great country of Spain. Would you, the Honorable Governor, give me a grant to the land?"

The governor was pleased with the gracious manners of the courteous Dubuque. It took little persuasion to get him to grant the same land with the same rights he had gotten from the Indians.

"You do me great honor," Dubuque told him as he prepared to leave. "I would like to honor you and your country by calling this grant 'The Mines of Spain'."

Now Dubuque worked twice as hard. More smelting furnaces were built. He kept looking for more lead ore back in the hills. The Indian women and the old men kept on breaking off the ore, putting it in baskets, and carrying it out on their backs.

There with the wooded hills behind, they buried Little Night.

For twenty-two years Dubuque lived among the Indians who were his friends. He mined and he traded. He seemed to be very successful.

Actually he did not know how to handle his business affairs. Twice a year he continued to go to St. Louis with boat loads of ore and furs, but he kept going deeper and deeper in debt. When he died, he was a poor man.

Dubuque's Death

As quickly as Dubuque's birch canoe had darted into Catfish Creek when he came bringing gifts to Kettle Chief, so he left them. He had come home one night with a hot skin and a pain in his chest. Anxiously Potosa and the other Indian women tried to relieve his pain. It was no use. Dubuque had pneumonia. By morning, Little Night had gone to the Happy Hunting Ground.

Kettle Chief spoke for his tribe. "Little Night was our brother," he said. "We will bury him like a brother."

58

The trolley car at Dubuque.

Kettle Chief and his village mourned deeply for Little Night. Chiefs and warriors from other villages came for miles around.

"Our hearts are heavy," they said. "Little Night was our friend too."

A sorrowful procession followed behind his body as they carried it up the winding path to the top of the high bluff overlooking the river. There, with the wooded hills behind, they buried Little Night. Just below was to be the city named for him—Dubuque. Lovingly they built a stone wall around the grave. Then the grave was covered with lead. At one end of the grave they placed a cedar cross, ten feet high.

The Sac and Fox visited his grave every year. Each Indian would throw a small stone on the grave. Over the years a huge pile of stones covered the spot.

Later, after the white men came and forced the Sac and Fox to leave their homes along the Mississippi, no one visited the grave.

In 1837 the city of Dubuque was built on the site of Kettle Chief's village. In 1897 a monument was built by the citizens of Dubuque to honor the man for whom the city was named. Today this tower stands as a reminder to anyone who looks up to the top of the bluff, of Julien Dubuque, the first white man to live in Iowa.

Chapter 6

MONUMENT UPON THE PRAIRIE

The big keelboat rubbed against the wharf with a grating whine. Ahead bobbed two flat-bottomed row-boats, piled high with bales of provisions: clothing, food, utensils, flints, powder and ball. The Missouri River flowed by gray and muddy.

"We're shoving off!" came a shout from shore.

The little camp on shore sprang to life. Soldiers, hunters, and roughly clad frontiersmen gathered excitedly at the wharf. All winter and most of the spring they had waited for just this moment.

"Yes, sir, Mr. Clark. We're really shoving off," repeated Old York as he shouldered his master's gear and headed for the boats. William Clark followed the Negro down to the landing. Even he could not hide the excitement that he felt at the announcement. Only the sober, scientific Captain Lewis appeared unmoved as he strode briskly from his headquarters, shouting orders to the men who were now pulling up the anchors and casting off the shore lines.

"Shove off! Keep those tow lines dry! And Sergeant Floyd. . ."

A young soldier with a ready smile snapped to attention.

"Captain Clark will be in charge here. I've got some business to finish up in St. Louis. I'll join you at St. Charles day after tomorrow."

"Yes, sir," replied the young sergeant, smartly.

Sergeant Charles Floyd was a Kentuckian. Some of the other soldiers jokingly called him the backwoods soldier, but Captain Lewis had recognized at once the qualities of a fine soldier in the young volunteer. For this reason he had selected the young Floyd to accompany him on this expedition and had commissioned him as one of the three sergeants.

It would be two years and four months before the little squat settlement of St. Louis would see again the 45 men of the Lewis and Clark Expedition. A varied crew they made that May morning as they shouldered the tow ropes and pulled the boats up the wide Missouri River. Fourteen were soldiers of the United States Army who had volunteered for the trip. Nine were young men from Kentucky; two were French watermen, long familiar with the trade routes down the Missouri to St. Louis.

The expedition had been President Thomas Jefferson's idea. He had just purchased the huge Louisiana Territory from Emperor Napoleon of France. He wanted to know what kind of a bargain he had made. He felt the best way to find out was to send someone to explore the area. What better man for such a mission than his old friend and neighbor, Meriwether Lewis?

All in all the expedition was a heroic undertaking. The men on the journey would have to make their way

CENTENNIAL EXPOSITION
PORTLAND, OREGON,
JUNE 1, 1905

The leaders of the Lewis and Clark Expedition

through thousands of miles of unknown regions, inhabited by uncivilized Indian tribes and live the best they could on whatever the wilderness might yield. From the expedition President Jefferson hoped to learn if the Missouri River provided a waterway to the Pacific Ocean, what the geography of the Territory was like, and what type of people inhabited the vast region.

By the time the boats were underway that May 14, 1804, it was 4 o'clock in the afternoon.

"We won't make more than four miles today," complained Moses Reed, a disgruntled soldier, who at this

63

point was not too sure he should have volunteered for such an adventure.

"We'll make better time when the wind swings around and we can hoist the square sail on the keelboat," encouraged Sergeant Floyd. The two men were walking along the shore, leading the only two horses that would accompany the expedition. In the middle of the river channel the boatmen were bent over their oars struggling against the swift current.

Sergeant Floyd was proud of his part in the expedition. His duties as sergeant were to watch for obstructions in the river that might hinder the boats and to keep a sharp lookout for enemy Indians lurking on shore. It would also be his responsibility to halt the expedition for rest and refreshments, guide the landing of the boats, and distribute food and water. At all times he had to locate mouths of rivers and creeks and warn of islands in the river channel.

Slowly up the wide Missouri toiled the expedition. Most of the time the men had to row, but when the wind blew from the right direction, the sails were hoisted. When the boats got snagged on sand bars and sunken logs, the men pulled from shore with the tow lines. Some of the men stayed in the boats while others hunted along the shore. At night the little group set up camp along the lonely shores of the big river. On one occasion the keelboat had run under an overhanging tree and broken the mast. At one time their boat nearly upset in the swift current, for the Missouri was running high.

The expedition had been traveling about fifteen days when they met two rafts loaded with furs and buffalo tallow bound for St. Louis from the Sioux Nations upstream. On one of the rafts was a French Creole named Old Dorion, who had lived with the Sioux Indians for twenty years. Clark saw at once that such a man would be a valuable asset on the trip. Without hesitation, he asked the Creole to join them. The possibility of a new adventure always appealed to Old Dorion, and he agreed to go along.

By July 18, the party had reached the southwest corner of the present state of Iowa. To the right of the men stretched the vast prairie meadows covered with the thick growth of waving grass. In the distance a high range of steep, treeless bluffs lined the horizon. As the expedition drew near the Iowa bank, a half starved dog tottered out from the underbrush. The men called to the dog and offered him some meat, which he gobbled up greedily. Some of the men tried to coax the dog to follow, but the animal snarled at them and staggered back into the Iowa prairie. That night, camping on the Nebraska side, the men sent out two hunters, who bagged two deer.

On July 21, the exploring party camped again on the Nebraska side opposite the present town of Glenwood. Clark left the camp and explored over on the Iowa side. He walked a mile back into the level bottom land, studying the Iowa soil and noting its fertility. That night a pack of wolves howled about the lonely camp, according to Clark's journal.

The next night the men camped for the first time on Iowa soil at a point where today the counties of Mills and Pottawattamie join.

"This is a good situation," announced Lewis. "We'll stay here a few days and dry out our provisions." The expedition had been drenched in heavy rains. The men were glad of a chance to rest.

"You, Drweyer and Peter Crousett," ordered Clark. "Take a pouch of tobacco and see if you can find any

Otoes. Give them the tobacco and ask them if they will come in and talk with us." Both Lewis and Clark realized that it was necessary to establish friendly relations with the Indians at once, for the success and safety of the little band of 45 men depended upon the friendliness of these tribes.

"Indians on this river are usually in the prairie hunting buffalo at this season," spoke up Old Dorion.

"That I know," argued Clark, "but from the signs we've seen—like that prairie fire yesterday—I think they just might be around."

The wind blew hard the four days that the men rested in Iowa. Poor Captain Clark was attempting to prepare papers and reports to send back to President Jefferson, but the wind blowing the sand made it impossible for him to work in his tent. He tried to write in the keelboat, but it pitched so violently that he gave up. Gathering up his papers, he stalked off into the woods, but here he had to fight off swarms of mosquitoes which had pestered the men during the hot summer trip. Clark finally gave up, and the papers were not sent until the expedition had reached the Mandan village in North Dakota. Later the men whom he had sent out to contact the Otoes returned, but reported that they could find no trace of Indians.

The party moved on up the river and camped for the second time in Iowaland about six miles above the mouth of Pigeon Creek, which Lewis named Indian Knob Creek. Here the men marveled at the evidences of a "Dreddfull harican" that had gone through about a year before. The storm had probably been an Iowa twister. Huge trees were broken off at the ground, and many had been torn from the earth by their roots.

Moving slowly on up the Missouri, the men passed

the point where the Boyer River joins the Missouri. One of the men, in trying to cross over at this point, let his gun fall into the water. A gun was a valuable possession in this wild land. One of the frontiersmen speedily dived into the current and rescued the gun.

The third camp in Iowa was nine miles north of the mouth of the Boyer River. Several days before, Lewis had found a white horse wandering around alone. The men had caught the animal and gladly added it to the other two horses of the expedition. When they awoke that morning in their Iowa camp, they found that their newly-acquired horse had died.

In his journal, Clark describes what he saw the next morning as he climbed the Nebraska bank of the Missouri and gazed across to Iowa:

". . . from the Bluff on the 2nd rise imediately above our Camp, the most butifull prospect of the River up & down the countrey opsed. Presented it Self which I ever beheld. The River meandering the open and butifull Plains, intespursed with Groves of timber, and each point covered with Tall timber, Such as Willow Cotton, sum Mulberry, Elm, Sucamore, Lynn, & ash. Two ranges of High Land parrelel to each other, and from 4 to 10 miles Distant, between which the river & its bottoms are Contained."

The next day a party of Oto and Missouri Indians were brought into camp. Lewis and Clark met and welcomed the Indians and arranged a meeting for the next day. As a present Lewis gave the Indians roast meat, pork, flour, and meal. The Indians, in turn, gave the white men watermelons. That night the expedition kept a close guard, for they were not too sure they could trust the Indians. No one was caught sleeping at his guard post that night, as had Alexander Willard a

A monument at Council Bluffs commemorates the council with the Indians of the Louisiana Territory.

couple of weeks before. For this Willard had received 100 lashes on his bare back. Captain Lewis had to keep strict discipline over his small band if they were to survive.

The Council with the Indians the next day was held under the shade of the sail of the keelboat. Lewis paraded his men before the Indian visitors and extended the good wishes of the United States Government for peace. He gave the chiefs clothes and medals, for the customary manner of recognizing a chief was to place a medal around the chief's neck. Each chief, upon receiving his medal, gave a speech telling how happy he was to learn about the Great White Father in Washington upon whom they could now depend. Captain Lewis, to amuse the visitors, shot off an air gun. The Indians were greatly astonished.

Clark named the first meeting place with the Indians of the Louisiana Territory, Council Bluffs. The Iowa city which grew up across the Missouri River from these bluffs still bears the name.

One of the men whom Lewis had sent after the Indians, a Frenchman named La Liberty, did not return to camp with the group.

"This man has evidently tired his horse or lost himself in the plains," said Lewis. He asked the Indians, before they departed from the council, to hunt for the lost man. That night Moses Reed asked permission to return to the site of the last night's camp to hunt for a knife which he had lost. Lewis let the man go back, but by nightfall the man had not returned. Lewis now had two men lost in the wild prairies of Iowa.

The fourth camp in Iowa was made just south of the mouth of the Soldier River. Clark went hunting wild turkey in Iowa that evening. He found large quantities of grapes along the river bank, but he also found large swarms of mosquitoes. The party began to think that Moses Reed, who had gone back for his knife, had deserted. As they camped for the fifth time in Iowa, just above the Soldier River, there was still no trace of the man.

Sometimes as the expedition traveled, they found themselves so near a point that they had just passed the day before that a man was sent to step across the land which separated the two camps to measure their progress. One time the man stepped 934 yards. The distance the party had covered by river was more than 18 miles.

On the next day the expedition camped six miles below the Little Sioux River, or the "Petite Riviere de Sioux" as the French trappers had termed it. French adventurers and trappers had often been in this region in search of furs and game. Old Dorion told Captain Lewis that this river rose not far from the west branch of the Des Moines River and that it passed through a lake 60 miles in circumference, which was divided into two parts. The lake was called "The Lake of the Great Spirit."

Captain Lewis decided that he had better try to locate his two lost men. He sent four soldiers back to look for Reed with instructions that "if he did not give up peacibly to put him to Death." They were also instructed to go back as far as the Oto village and ask if the Indians had found the Frenchman, La Liberty.

The seventh Iowa camp was located within the southwest corner of Monona County. Clark took one man and walked back into the wilds of Iowa. The man killed an elk, but Clark fired four times and had to return to camp empty handed. He wrote in his journal that night, "The ball being Small, I think was the reason."

As they walked through the unexplored Iowa land, the mosquitoes were so thick that Clark picked off a part of a bush to swat the insects, but even with this weapon, he could not keep them out of his eyes. Clark commented that night: "Mosquitoes turrible. . . but snakes are not plenty in this part."

The group camped next near Whiting, Iowa. Here, after they had pitched camp and were trying to get to sleep, a prairie wolf came near the bank and barked. He sounded like a large, fierce dog. The men got up and tried to catch the animal, but they could not get near him. One of Lewis and Clark's duties on the expedition was to report on the kind of animal life which existed in the Territory.

Two days later the men who had been sent back for the two deserters returned, accompanied by three Oto chiefs. They were leading the deserter, Moses Reed, but La Liberty, the Frenchman, had deceived them and got away. Desertion from an army expedition was a serious offense. The captain knew he must punish the man. After a brief council with the visiting Indian chiefs, Lewis proceeded to the punishment.

Confronted with the evidence, Moses Reed mumbled, "I confess I deserted and stol'd a rifle, short pouch, powder and ball."

"You know the consequences?" asked Lewis.

Reed hung his head. "Yes. But Captain. Go easy on me."

Lewis let the men of the expedition vote on the punishment due the deserter.

"You are sentenced to run the gauntlet four times with each man allowed to switch you nine times, and hereafter you are not to be considered a member of the expedition."

The Oto chief shook his head when the sentence of punishment was translated to him.

"Too hard," he protested. "White man sorry. Pardon man."

Lewis knew that Reed must be made an example to the rest of the men. He could not risk having his soldiers desert in the middle of an 8,000-mile mission.

"It is the custom of our country," Lewis explained to the chief. "This man has done a great wrong against his Great White Father. He must be punished."

The chief nodded his head.

The punishment of Reed was carried out as the chiefs watched. After disposing of this business, the men turned toward lighter amusements. It was the birthday of one of the men of the expedition. In celebration they danced until 11 o'clock.

The next morning Lewis gave the Indians presents, and they mounted their ponies and departed. The festivities of the night before were quickly forgotten, for as Clark reports in his journal: "sergeant Floyd is taken verry bad all at once."

The expedition had no doctor. Captain Clark looked down on the young man as he lay on his bed roll, doubled up in pain.

71

"It's bilious colic. Probably from drinking the muddy water."

The men nodded soberly.

"Stay with him through the night. All we can do is try to relieve him of the pain," ordered the Captain calmly, but he was alarmed at the situation. He could not afford to lose the services of a young man of Sergeant Floyd's caliber.

When morning came to the little camp, Sergeant Floyd was much weaker and no better. The men carried him to the keelboat, and the expedition set out under a gentle southeast breeze. As they crawled around two islands near the Iowa side, they saw a tall bluff looming ahead. As they drew near the bluff, Sergeant Floyd called out weakly to Captain Clark, "I am going away. I want you to write me a letter." His voice grew fainter. The men turned sadly away.

The soldiers buried Sergeant Floyd with full military honors on the top of the lonely bluff, just a half a mile below a point where a small river joined the Missouri. Lewis placed a red cedar post at the head of the grave on which he had inscribed:

Sergeant C. Floyd
died here 20th of August, 1804

Captain Lewis turned to his men and said, "This man at all times gave us proof of his firmness and determined resolution to do service to his country and honor to himself." He turned quickly and strode off down the bluff.

That night the men camped at the mouth of the little river nearby. They agreed to name the river, the Floyd River, and the bluff where the brave sergeant was buried, Sergeant Bluff. The names remain today. Half a

The Floyd monument at Sioux City marks the grave of the first American soldier to be buried in Iowa soil.

century later, the city of Sioux City was laid out near the spot where Floyd was buried.

The next day the Lewis and Clark Expedition left Iowaland and followed the route of the Missouri River as it veered off into the present state of South Dakota. The group spent the winter with the Mandan Indians in North Dakota. They ascended the Missouri River to its source, went down the Columbia River in the great Northwest, and spent the next winter near its mouth. Coming back, the party divided, some going on down the Yellowstone River and others down the Missouri River. The two groups reunited below the mouth of the Yellowstone and began the return trip down the Missouri.

On September 4th, two years and one month after leaving Iowaland, the Lewis and Clark Expedition returned. When they reached the high bluff where Sergeant Floyd was buried, they climbed up to pay their respects to their lost friend. They found that someone had molested the grave. They refilled the grave, replaced the marker, and passed on down the Great Muddy. In five days the men had passed the southwest corner of Iowa—a distance that had taken them over a month to travel on the way upstream. Late in September, the Lewis and Clark Expedition entered St. Louis, fired a salute from the swivel gun mounted on the keelboat, and went ashore to receive a welcome from the whole village.

The expedition had cost the life of but one man, but there had been no other serious casualties. During the years that followed, the cedar post that Lewis had placed on the grave of Sergeant Floyd as a marker was often lost by prairie fires sweeping over the bluff or by the erosion of the soil along the river bank. Travelers often replaced the marker as they journeyed up the Missouri. For many years the post served as a landmark to early traders and Indians as well.

Today a large stone slab covers the grave of Sergeant Floyd, and towering 100 feet above is a tall stone needle

—a monument upon the prairie to the first white man to die and be buried on Iowa soil.

The Lewis and Clark Expedition became the first publicity agent for the new Louisiana Territory. The journals kept by the two leaders marked the beginning of knowledge concerning Iowa and sparked the first interest in the land between the two great rivers. Because of Captain Lewis and William Clark, good will between the white and red man was established. Iowa never became a battleground between the two races.

Chapter 7

PIKE FINDS A PEAK

"Rapids ahead!"

Lieutenant Zebulon Pike scrambled to the front of the 70-foot keelboat and peered ahead. As far as he could see, the Mississippi River bubbled and churned in a series of fast flowing rapids.

"Shift the cargo," he ordered. "We'll try to get through!"

The first 230 miles up river from St. Louis had been navigated with little or no difficulty, but these rapids looked dangerous. Lieutenant Pike grasped the tiller firmly as the boat tossed in the rough water.

The Pike Expedition

He had to make good on this expedition. He could not see all his plans and preparations of the past summer destroyed now, just as the expedition was getting into the most important part of the mission. General James H. Wilkinson, the head of the United States Army, had selected Zebulon Pike to head the 20 man crew with instructions to explore to the source of the Mississippi

River and to make recommendations for the establishment of forts along its shores. It was an important task for the 26-year old officer.

Zeb Pike had been in the army almost as long as he could remember. He was born in New Jersey while his father had been away fighting in the Revolutionary War. Zeb had enlisted at the age of fifteen, and now at twenty-six he was a fine American officer. He was of medium height, was strong and wiry, and had light curly hair and sparkling blue eyes.

He could never forget his excitement at being summoned into General Wilkinson's office last June and told that he had been chosen to head the Mississippi expedition. General Wilkinson had told him that he must find out everything he could about this part of the newly acquired Louisiana Territory: How far was the Mississippi navigable? What was the attitude of the Indian tribes toward the Americans? What was the land like? The general had told him that this region had long known French and English traders, but that it would be Pike's duty to win the loyalty of the Indians over to the American government, which now owned the land. General Wilkinson also thought it would be advisable to watch for good sites for military forts that could be used to protect the United States' hold upon the new land.

The expedition had started up the Mississippi from St. Louis, August 9, 1805, and here they were at the Des Moines River Rapids on August 20—just one year to the day that Sergeant Floyd had died on the Lewis and Clark Expedition on the opposite side of Iowa.

Rescue on the Rapids

"We made that one!" shouted one of the soldiers from the prow. But looming ahead was more of the same raging water. The keelboat bobbed and tumbled in the current. Pike wondered if he dared risk trying to get through the next rapids.

"Canoes off starboard!" shouted the soldier. "And they're waving a United States flag!"

Pike turned. Several canoes were threading their way cautiously through the rapids toward the floundering keel. Two white men were in the lead canoe. Behind were several more canoes of Indians.

"I'm William Ewing, United States Agricultural Agent at the Indian village over there," announced the white man as he clambered on board. "And this is young Tesson."

"Honore's son?" asked Pike.

The young Frenchman nodded.

The name Tesson was not unknown to Pike. He had been told of the three Spanish land grants along the Mississippi. Everyone on the frontier had heard of Tesson and his apple orchard. Honore Tesson had bought 6073 acres of land in 1799 when the land west of the Mississippi was still owned by Spain. He had moved his family into this unknown wilderness and returned to St. Louis, where he purchased large quantities of young apple trees. With the bundles of young trees strapped on the back of his pack mules, he had made his way back to his land and planted his farm to apple orchard. Here Tesson and his family lived and traded with the Indians for furs, existing on whatever they could hunt and trap. It was a wild kind of life for a white boy.

"We saw you were having trouble," Ewing continued, "but I think we can get you through."

At Ewing's advice the men moved the barrels of cargo into the canoes—barrels of flour, corn meal, pork, gunpowder, salt, tobacco along with blankets, tents, and numerous presents for the Indians.

With the weight of the boat lessened, Pike steered through the eleven miles of rapids, following the canoes as they darted through the dangerous shoals, which today are the site of the Keokuk Dam.

After fighting the rapids for several hours, Pike and his men were only too glad to spend the night with Ewing at the Indian village. In the morning they went across the river to visit another Indian village, located on land now occupied by the town of Montrose. Pike took young Tesson along to act as an interpreter.

The Indian village contained about thirteen lodges, some of them as long as 100 feet. The frames were made of poles and covered with a sheathing of elm bark fastened with thongs of buckskin. Buffalo skins hung from the doorways, and in the center of the lodges were fire pits. On frames along the sides were beds made of skins of animals stretched over poles.

Through young Tesson, Pike explained to the Indian chiefs the object of his trip. "I come in peace from your Great Father. He has sent me to find out your needs and to tell you that he will protect you." This was the first information that the Indians had received that their hunting grounds west of the Mississippi now belonged to the United States. Pike gave the Indians presents of tobacco and knives from his barrels of provisions. The Indians signed no treaties, but Pike left feeling that the Indians would be friendly to any settlers that might come into the new land.

The Expedition Moves On

When it was time for the expedition to be on their way, young Tesson watched wistfully as the keelboat pulled away from shore and started its slow journey up river.

The next night Pike and his men camped near the present city of Fort Madison. Four years later the first fort in Iowa would be erected at this point. Pike, however, did not think the site good enough to recommend that a fort be built here. He thought the site of the next night's camp as more suitable for this purpose. This location was near the present city of Burlington. Pike wrote in his journal: "There is a hill which rises up perpendicularly to a height of about 60 feet. On the summit is a level platform of about four hundred yards. In the rear is a small prairie of about eight or ten acres suitable for garden. This would be a very good place for a garrison."

Lost on the Prairie

The next day Pike and one of his men took two dogs and went ashore to hunt. It was a hot, sultry day. When the two men were ready to return to the keelboat, they could not find their dogs. Pike hated to lose these dogs for they were two of his favorites. Two of the men volunteered to go back and find the animals. The expedition waited on the shore for the men to return. It was a well known rule of the expedition that the keelboat did not wait for anyone. When it was time to continue, Pike regretfully left the men. That night at their camp a few miles up river, Pike shot off a gun every hour to guide the lost men, but morning came and the men had not returned.

Pike Meets Black Hawk

As the expedition moved up the river, they saw another Indian village of considerable size on the east side of the river. This was Saukenuk, the home of the great Sac and Fox chief, Black Hawk. Black Hawk had just returned from leading a war party against one of the enemy tribes. Pike came ashore dressed in his brightest military uniform. He greeted the great chieftain politely in French, for Black Hawk could speak the French language as well as his own Indian language.

"I am happy to meet you here in this council fire, which your father, President Jefferson, has sent me to kindle and to take you by the hands as our children." Pike was well versed in how to treat the Indians. He treated them as politely as he did any white man. He never threatened them but always made himself one of them, sleeping in their lodges, eating their food, and talking with their warriors. He told Black Hawk that all the Indian tribes were the Great Father's children and that they must live together in peace.

Black Hawk was impressed by the polite young army officer. He took the flag which the American gave him. Pike suggested that perhaps Black Hawk would like to take down the British flag which was flying above his village. Black Hawk refused. "Sac and Fox will be friends to both fathers," stated the wily chief.

Leaving the village of Saukenuk, Pike and his men visited another Indian village on the Iowa side, hoping to find some trace of the lost men, but none of the Sac and Fox had seen the men. Sadly they continued their trip, fearing that their companions were hopelessly lost on the Iowa prairie.

A Surprise at the Lead Mines of Dubuque

The next Sunday they reached the lead mines of Spain, the home of Julien Dubuque. Dubuque, seeing the expedition making its way up the river, fired a salute from a cannon. He graciously invited the men to stay at his settlement. Pike was anxious to find out just how extensive the lead deposits were in this part of Iowa. He attempted to question Dubuque, but the miner did not want to answer the questions. He feared that the United States Government might want to take the lead mines from him.

Pike asked if he might visit the mines, but Dubuque assured him that they were too far distant to walk and there just happened to be no horses available for the trip. Lieutenant Pike felt that he should examine the mines, but he became sick with a fever before he could do so. He prepared a list of questions for Dubuque to answer, but he learned little more from the clever Frenchman:

What is the date of your grant for the mines from the savages?

The copy of the grants is in Mr. Soulard's office at St. Louis.

What is the date of the confirmation by the Spaniards?

The same as to your query first.

What is the extent of your grant?

The same as above.

But the visit with Dubuque was not all disappointment. While the men were enjoying the hospitality of the French miner, a canoe arrived with the two missing soldiers of the expedition on board. The men reported that they had wandered around on the prairies for six days with nothing to eat but some mussels, a type of clam, which they found along the river bank. They had finally wandered into the camp of a fur trader who had given them some food and taken them to an Indian village. Here they had met Maurice Blondeau, a French fur trader and interpreter from Montrose. Blondeau had offered to help them catch up with their companions.

A view of the Mississippi River from the bluffs of Iowa

Pike now realized that in order to talk to the various Indian tribes, he needed an interpreter. Blondeau agreed to accompany the expedition.

Pike Finds a Peak

As they passed the mouth of the Turkey River, the men decided to go ashore. Pike writes in his journal: "In the course of the day, we landed to shoot pigeons. The moment a gun was fired, some Indians, who were on the shore above us, ran down and put off in their perogues[2] with great precipitation." Pike had been told by Blondeau that all the women and children were frightened at the very name of an American boat. The Sioux Indians of this region held Americans in great respect, considering them "very quarrelsome, much for war, and also very brave." This idea had been instilled

[2] Perogues or pirogues are dugout canoes or any canoelike boat.

in them by the British fur traders, who still held many forts in the Great Lakes region and had not given up hope of extending their own claims in the new land.

The next stop was at the Wisconsin settlement of Prairie du Chien, located on the east side of the Mississippi where the Wisconsin River enters the larger stream. This settlement consisted of eighteen houses. Some of the houses were frame, but most of them were made of logs, daubed with mud on the outside and white-washed on the inside. On the Iowa side were three houses clustered on the shores of a small stream called the Giard River.

Giard was also a familiar name to Pike. Giard was the third white man who held the title of his land from an old Spanish grant. His land consisted of 5680 acres of land in Clayton County, just across from Prairie du Chien.

On September 4, Pike reports that he "breakfasted below the Wisconsin at Prairie du Chien, and at 11 a.m. set out to look for a site for a fort." He crossed to the Iowa side and climbed a high hill. Here he found a level plateau from which he could see the Mississippi River with its many bayous stretching for miles in either direction. The hill was make up of a variety of colored sands. Pike described the spot as "a commanding spot, level on top, a spring in the rear, most suitable for a military post." He made detailed drawings of the spot and recommended that a fort be erected here. Today the spot is known as Pike's Peak State Park and the view remains as untouched and as wild as the day Pike stood upon it and gazed up and down the great river below. Before Pike could return to his camp that day, "a shower of rain came up which completely wet us and we returned to the village within an hour."

84

Pike left his keelboat at Prairie du Chien and transferred to two flat bottomed boats. Just above Prairie du Chien near the Upper Iowa River, he received a welcome from a group of Sioux Indians, who had a village there. The Indians had been celebrating the night before. When they saw Pike approaching in his two boats, they tried to see how close they could shoot at the boats without hitting the men. Pike was escorted to their chief, Wabasha. He smoked the peace pipe with the Sioux chief, and the warriors presented a medicine dance for the white men. In return Pike gave the Indians presents from their new White Father.

The Expedition Ends

At this point Pike left Iowa. He continued up to the headwaters of the Mississippi, spending the winter in Minnesota. When the ice had gone from the rivers, he started home. Floating leisurely down the river in the early spring, Pike met several boats coming upstream "under full sail." He was most happy to receive a letter through one of the boatmen from his wife and small daughter, who had remained in St. Louis during the nine months of the expedition.

During his 500 mile journey, Pike had seen only three white settlements on the upper Mississippi, all in Iowa. They were the three Spanish grants: Tesson's Apple Orchard, Dubuque's Mines of Spain, and Giard's farm in Clayton County. Pike arrived in St. Louis April 20, 1806.

Zeb Pike had more than carried out his orders. He had made friends with nearly 30 tribes of Indians, many of whom were not overjoyed to welcome Americans. The British had long been active among the Indians of this region stirring up dislike for the Americans and

The Zebulon Pike Memorial at Burlington

courting their favor with goods far superior to those traded by the Americans. Pike had inspired the Indians with respect for America and had discovered the extent of British trade. He was an accurate reporter and gave the first good account of this upper Mississippi region which helped popularize eastern Iowa and prepared the way for permanent settlement.

As for the proposed forts at Burlington and on Pike's Peak, his advice was never heeded. In all, the expedition was a success, with the loss of only two dogs.

With the Indians

For many years the red man roamed across Iowa, happy and content, untouched by cultures developing in other parts of the world. Late in the 17th century, bearded outlanders, or so the Indians called the first French fur traders, began to venture across the Great River bringing with them customs from their European homeland.

An early map of 1703 shows a trail used by these French fur traders, running from the Mississippi River near the mouth of the Wisconsin River across northern Iowa, through the Spirit Lake region to the Big Sioux River. This trail was known to the French as the *Chemin des Voyageurs*. With the coming of these first French fur traders, two cultures met in Iowa: the highly developed European culture and the primitive Indian culture. It would not be long before the European would overpower the Indian.

The early French fur traders found it wise to adopt many of the Indian ways in order to survive in the new wild land. In turn, the Indians were attracted by many things which the European brought in. A type of commerce was set up. The Indians found they could trade furs for iron tools, traps, guns, bright-colored blankets, and cloth, but in the trade the Indians were to find that they had received some less desirable items that would help eventually to destroy them: whiskey and disease.

Chapter 8

FROM WOODLANDS AND PLAINS

When the French explorers, Marquette and Joliet, came to Iowa in 1673, the Indians whom they met along the Mississippi River were Algonquin or Woodland Indians. Because these Indians liked to hunt and fish, they lived close to the woods and rivers.

The prairies of Iowa acted as a barrier between these Woodland Indians and another distinctly different group roaming east of the Missouri River, called the Sioux or Plains Indians. It is thought that the Algonquins came from the north and east and the Sioux from the north and west. The names, Algonquin and Sioux, probably came from the most important tribe within each group. Both the Algonquin and Sioux Indians came in search of food, conquering or driving out the smaller tribes. The two Indian groups met in Iowa making this land a battleground and hunting area between them. Probably the two groups did not total more than 12,000 people.

The Algonquin group was composed of the Sac and Fox, Potawatomi, and the Mascoutin tribes. The group also included the Iowa, who were of Sioux ancestry but had adopted the ways of the Woodland Indians.

The Sioux group included the Oto, Missouri, Omaha, Winnebago, and the hostile Sioux. Besides these two large groups, there were many other Indian tribes that passed through Iowa after being forced from their lands by the white settlers in the east, but these did not settle in Iowa.

When the United States purchased the Louisiana Territory in 1803, the Sac and Fox tribe was living along the Mississippi River while the Iowas were living along the Des Moines River. The Missouri, Oto, and Omaha lived along the Missouri River, and the Sioux tribe lived along the Big Sioux and upper Des Moines rivers. White settlers had contact mostly with the Sac and Fox, some dealings with the Iowa, very little with the Missouri, Oto, and Omaha, and no contact with the Sioux until 50 years later.

The Woodland Indians

The Sac and Fox of the Woodland culture were, perhaps, the most advanced of any of the Indian tribes living in Iowa. Some historians believe that they were on the verge of making a great step toward civilization when the white man came. They had a well-organized type of government, a literature, and a type of drama, but they had not yet discovered anything mechanical.

The Sac and Fox had been two separate tribes at one time. The Iroquis Indians, together with the French fur traders, had forced them from their homes in Michigan and Wisconsin. The Fox tribe had been nearly destroyed in the many battles. About the time the white men were beginning to come into Iowa, the two tribes joined forces and moved down the Mississippi River.

A wickiup of the Woodland Indians

These Indians lived in villages and farmed the surrounding land. Their main crops were corn, beans, pumpkins, and tobacco. They lived in wickiups made of strips of bark and mats of woven cattails, spread over a framework of poles which were bent and stuck into the ground. These wickiups had no windows and only one door. In the winter the door was covered with an animal skin. In the middle of the wickiup, the Indian women built a fire on which the meals were prepared. The smoke escaped through a hole in the roof. The wickiups were dark and smoky, but quite warm. Around the sides of the shelter were piles of skins on which the family slept.

Families within the Sac and Fox group were organized into clans which bore such names as Wolf, Bear, Dog, and Elk. Several clans made up a tribe. Each tribe was ruled by a head chief, assisted by a council made up of older members of the tribe. Although the position of head chief was inherited, a warrior could become a war chief if he were outstanding in battle.

Sac and Fox Warriors

Indian men spent a great amount of time hunting and fishing. During the summer months of June, July, and August, they left the village for the summer hunt, while the women stayed at home to care for the growing crops. The winter hunt was different. Everyone could go along. The women and children busily harvested the crops, then left with the men. They would be gone until the planting time in the spring. It was exciting as they traveled along the rivers in canoes fashioned from skins of animals.

Often the thoughts of the warriors were of war. If no one were organizing a war party in his own village, a warrior might join with another village. Before going to war, the warrior would blacken his face, fast for several days, neglecting his appearance until he felt that the Great Spirit was pleased. Since the life span of the Indian was not long, Indian men were considered old at 45. At that time his sons took over his place in the tribe.

Sac and Fox Women

While the Indian men provided for their families by hunting and fishing and showed their bravery in battle, the women took care of the villages. Carefully each Indian woman planned her work, for there was much to do. Tanning hides, gathering wood, carrying water, preparing meals, weaving mats, and caring for the children were all a part of her responsibility. She planted the crops with care and tended them faithfully. For a hoe, she used a pointed stick with a stone or clam shell attached to the end. She watched anxiously for the rains to come. She feared a drought or an early frost, for she knew her people might starve if there were not a good crop. When the harvesting was done, she looked proudly at the corn as she ground it into meal between two stones and stored it in bags made of bark or animal skins. Now she knew her family would live well during the winter, even if the hunt was poor.

The Indian woman worked hard every day, but she enjoyed her work. She married young, probably around the age of 15. She kept her baby close by her as she worked. Usually it was in a hammock-like cradle which could be hung inside the wickiup or strapped to the mother's back as she prepared food for a meal. The Indians ate whenever they were hungry, the men eating first and the woman and children eating what was left. There were no tables nor chairs. Everyone sat around a kettle placed in the center.

When the women were not busy growing or preparing the food, they tanned the skins of animals and sewed them into garments, using a needle made of bone. The Sac and Fox made their garments of doe skin or skins of other animals found along the wooded streams.

Women held a place of honor in the Algonquin tribes. Houses, furnishings, and gardens were owned by the Indian women. The warriors owned only their hunting equipment.

Sac and Fox Children

When the Sac and Fox children were small, the mother trained them. Indians never whipped their children. If a child were to be punished, his mother might blacken his face with charcoal and send him out of the wickiup. Indian children seldom cried and seldom smiled. Very few of them died of disease until after the white man came.

The Indian boys were raised to become warriors. At about the age of six, the boy was given a small bow and arrow and was allowed to hunt birds. Later he listened carefully as his father instructed him how to hunt the larger animals. An Indian boy had to learn many things before he could become a warrior: how to make a bow and a stone arrowhead, how to tell what the weather would be, how to use a tomahawk, and how to follow the tracks of man and animal. If he learned his lessons well, he was given a name telling of something he had done. An Indian boy tried to be very brave so that he would always be proud of his name. When the boy was fifteen and had demonstrated his ability, he was considered old enough to accompany the warriors on the war path.

The mother taught the Indian girl the things that she would need to know to be the good wife of a brave warrior: to skin the animals, tan the hides, fashion the hides into garments, move the wickiups, build the fires, and do the field work.

The Sioux Indians

While the Algonquins built their villages along the streams of eastern Iowa, the fierce Sioux roamed the western part of the state. The woods and streams of the Algonquins held no lure for the Sioux, for they lived, like the buffalo they hunted, on the open prairie. They were excellent horsemen. Because they were constantly on the move, they often had to fight with other tribes whose hunting grounds they invaded. This made them quarrelsome and cruel. Other tribes feared the Sioux. It

The Sioux Indians lived a nomadic life.

is said of the Sioux, "They fought fiercely and died bravely."

The Sioux depended upon the buffalo, which roamed across the prairie in huge herds, for their food, clothing, and shelter. While the Algonquin made his clothes from the hides of small animals such as the beaver and deer, the Sioux tanned and cured the tough hides of the buffalo. His house was a tepee made of buffalo hides sewed together and held up by a framework of poles. Such a home was easily taken down and carried along on the hunt by dragging the shelter sled-like on its poles.

The Sioux were ruled by a chief and a council, but they did not have clans as did the Sac and Fox. Living the nomadic life did not encourage strong family ties. The Sioux grouped together in bands, which might consist of members of several families.

The Indians Lose Iowa

Soon after the Louisiana Purchase, the white man moved into Iowa. In many ways the Indian and the white man did not understand each other. The red man did not view the ownership of the land in the same way as the white settler. The Indian thought that his tiny gardens and the ground on which to hunt were, by law of nature, his. Fences and titles meant nothing. He lived on the land, and, therefore, the land was his even though he might choose to roam the length of the state throughout the rest of the year.

In the customs of their culture, if an Indian buried his dead on the land, it became his land. If the Indian conquered another tribe's land, he hastened to bury his dead warriors there in order to establish his claim. One can well understand how an Indian might have felt when a white settler claimed the land where his tribe had buried his dead. The Indian felt that the white man spoiled the land with his cultivated fields and fences. The white man thought the Indian was a troublesome hindrance to his settlement.

Treaties meant little to the Indians. They did not understand white man's laws. They could not read nor write, and sometimes they could not understand what the white man was trying to say. Boundaries drawn up in the treaties were not always clear. Sometimes the Indians were paid partly in merchandise and partly in money for their land. Sometimes they were not paid at all. But for a time the selling of the land did not worry the Indian. There was always more land farther west, or so the Indian thought.

To help the Indian understand the ways of the white man, the United States Government appointed white Indian agents to live with the Indians and to teach them the ways of the white settlers. These agents were to keep peace among the various Indian tribes, to see that white traders did not cheat the Indians, and to represent the United States Government as a friend of the Indian. There were never more than two or three agents in Iowa at any one time. Some of them, such as Joseph M. Street, were honest, dedicated men and greatly loved by the Indians. Others, less honorable, cheated the Indians out of the money they received for their lands and kept them well supplied with whiskey.

How the White Man Got Control of the Land

Step by step the Indians were moved westward across Iowa in a series of treaties and purchases.

HALF-BREED TRACT—1824

The Indians did not want the white man on the west side of the Mississippi River. The first concession the

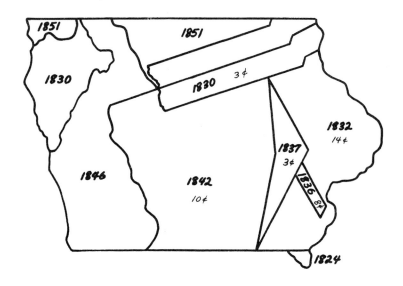

Step by step the Red Man lost his Iowa hunting grounds

Indians made was to allow white men who had married Indian women to settle in the southeast part of what is now Lee County. This came to be known as Half-Breed Land. By 1824 the white men had traded the Indians out of this land.

NEUTRAL STRIP—1830

The warlike Sioux were constantly making war on the more peaceful tribes. The Government in Washington suggested that a council of all tribes be called at Fort Crawford in Prairie du Chien. From this council came an agreement to establish a Neutral Strip running from the Upper Iowa River to the Des Moines River. The Sioux agreed to stay north of the line, the Sac and Fox south of the line. In 1830, the Government purchased the 40-mile strip for 3c an acre.

WESTERN SLOPE—1830

In the same year the Government purchased the entire western part of the present state of Iowa from the Sac and Fox, Omahas, Sioux, Oto, and the Missouri, paying each tribe whatever their claim in the area was. Supposedly it was to be kept as a hunting ground for the Indians. This area was referred to as the Western Slope.

THE BLACK HAWK PURCHASE—1832

After the Black Hawk War, the government purchased a strip of land about 50 miles wide just west of the Mississippi River from the Neutral Strip on south to the Missouri state line. The Indians received 14c an acre for this land.

KEOKUK'S RESERVE—1836

Keokuk, because of his role as peacemaker, was awarded a large expanse of land along the Iowa River. In 1836 the Indians sold this to the United States for 8c an acre.

SECOND BLACK HAWK PURCHASE—1837

As settlers continued to pour into Iowa, the Government needed even more land. In 1837 the United States again purchased a tract of land just west of the first Black Hawk Purchase for 3c an acre.

THE NEW PURCHASE—1842

Finally the Sac and Fox gave up the last of their land in Iowa and agreed to move to a reservation in Kansas. They were paid 10c an acre for this land which included most of central Iowa.

MISSOURI SLOPE—1846

Only three tribes now remained in Iowa: the Sioux, Winnebago, and Potawatomi. In 1846, the Potawatomi and Winnebago gave up their land on the Missouri slope east of the Little Sioux and Missouri rivers. The Potawatomi then joined the Sac and Fox in Kansas. The Winnebagoes moved to Minnesota.

SIOUX TRACT—1851

The Sioux were the last to give up their land in Iowa. In 1851 they signed a treaty to sell what is now the northwest corner of Iowa and a narrow strip along the present northern boundary of the state.

In less than 30 years' time the Indians had given up all claim to their land in Iowa. Although 3c to 10c per acre does not sound like a fair price today, it must be remembered that France had sold the entire Louisiana Territory for 5c an acre. The 3 million dollars that the United States Government paid the Indians for Iowa was over and above the money already paid to France for the same land.

The land was undeveloped at the time of these purchases. Neither the Indian nor the white settler knew how valuable the land might become some day—not as hunting ground as the Indian would have used it—but as rich, agricultural soil. But all in all, the price paid the Indian was probably the going price for land at the time.

The Indians reacted in different ways to the loss of their land. Black Hawk resisted. Keokuk compromised. Inkpaduta found his revenge in a massacre. The Mesquakies returned to Iowa and bought the land.

You will read about all of these in the next chapters.

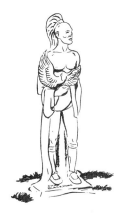

Chapter 9

BLACK HAWK—THE OLD
WAR CHIEF

"Our fellow tribesmen have returned from St. Louis," the Indian announced to the chiefs assembled in the Sac and Fox village of Saukenuk.

"Tell them to come. We have waited many days for their return." Quickly the chiefs gathered to hear the long-awaited report.

Five braves, two of whom were chiefs, had been sent to the white man's government because an Indian had killed a white man. The Indians had followed tribal law and taken the murderer to the white officials. They believed they could get their tribesman released by paying for the white man who had been killed.

While the braves were trying to make arrangements to get the prisoner released, a new governor, William Henry Harrison, arrived in St. Louis. Governor Harrison had received orders from the Government in Washington to make treaties with the Sac and Fox to get them to sell some of their land.

"We saw the American father," the spokesman began, "and told him why we had come. We asked for our brother."

"And where is our brother?" asked one of the chiefs. "Did he return with you?"

"No," replied the Indian. "He is not with us, for he is dead. He was shot when they let him out of prison."

"Did you not pay the money for his release?" demanded the chief.

"We paid no money," answered the brave. "The American father told us that he wanted land, not money. We were told by a trader friend that our brother would be released if we would sell some land."

"Land!" Chief Black Hawk entered the conversation. "What land?"

"We are not certain," answered the Indian, "but it was land on both sides of the Great River."

"You cannot sell land!" shouted Black Hawk. "Land cannot be sold except by the tribal council. What makes you think you sold land?"

"Forgive us, Chief Black Hawk, but we did sell land. We touched the goose quill and the land was sold."

The sound of angry voices rose from the council. Of all the chiefs, Black Hawk was the most angry.

"You had no right to sell our land," he declared. "I for one will never allow the white man to take our homes."

Keokuk had been sitting quietly, listening to Black Hawk's angry words and deciding in his clever mind what kind of action he should take.

When he spoke, his words were smooth and cunning.

The old war chief

"We should agree to the treaty," he announced. "Then the American father will take care of us."

Black Hawk turned angrily to Keokuk. "Is that all your homeland means to you?" he demanded. "Are you willing to give up your land for some horses and blankets and food? If so, go to the west side of the river. I do not wish to stay in the same village with you!"

The Treaty of 1804

The story was true as reported by the braves to the council. For the sum of $2,234.50 worth of goods and a $1,000 payment a year, the Sac and Fox chiefs had sold fifty-one million acres of land. This was all the land that the Sac and Fox claimed on the east side of the Mississippi.

The year that the treaty was signed was 1804. Black Hawk's troubles with the white man began with the signing of this treaty. Many years were to pass before the troubles were over.

Black Hawk left the council and went to his favorite spot, a high bluff overlooking the Rock River. He went there often to smoke and to think. It had become known as Black Hawk's Watch Tower. From this high bluff the entire Mississippi Valley could be seen. He sat and watched the Great River as it flowed endlessly to the south. He looked at the abundance of the land. He looked at his village below him. The familiar feeling of love for this beautiful land swept over him.

As he sat smoking, a decision began to form in Black Hawk's mind. This was his home and the home of his ancestors. This was going to stay his home and the home of his people for as long as he could fight for it. The white man and his government were not going to force him off this land that was rightfully the land of the Sac and Fox. He would wait for his chance to act against the white man's government.

The Building of Fort Madison

The chance came in 1808 when the Government sent soldiers to build a fort nine miles above the rapids on the Mississippi River. Lieutenant Kingsley was sent along with fifty soldiers to do the building.

The British traders had helped stir up the feeling of hatred that the Indians had for the Americans. British traders had told them that the Americans were plotting to take all of the Indian land.

"You cannot build a fort here," Black Hawk told the lieutenant. "You are building on our land."

"We aren't building a fort. We are building a house for a trader," Lieutenant Kingsley told him. "He is coming here to live. He will sell you goods very cheap. The soldiers are here to keep him company."

"We know the truth," Black Hawk answered. "A trader does not need so many buildings. Stop your building and go back down the river."

The lieutenant knew the Indians were getting hostile. He hurriedly opened up a trading post, but he did not fool the Indians. They laughed at the goods he offered them as they left to go to their winter hunting grounds.

The soldiers took advantage of the Indians' absence to get the fort completed. By April, 1809, the fort was finished with a stockade fourteen feet high surrounding it. It was called Fort Madison in honor of the new President of the United States.

An Attempt To Destroy Fort Madison

Meanwhile the Indians were spending their winter planning to destroy the fort. The plan was to go to the fort and ask permission to dance for the soldiers. Weapons would be concealed under their blankets. When they were all inside the fort, a signal would be given, and they would kill the soldiers.

One warm day in May of 1809, the Indians came to Fort Madison. While one chief was asking permission for the warriors to dance in the fort, Black Hawk was getting everyone around the gate ready to enter.

Permission was given, and the gate opened, but when the warriors started to go in they saw a cannon in front of the gateway and a soldier standing by ready to fire.

They had been betrayed! Someone had warned the soldiers of their plot. There was nothing they could do but leave, but Black Hawk and his warriors did not forget about their plan. If the fort could not be destroyed this time, it could be another.

The Burning of Fort Madison

During the War of 1812, the war the Americans fought against the British, Black Hawk joined the British army. His feeling of being wronged by the American Government had increased with the building of Fort Madison. It was during this war that the next chance came to destroy the fort.

When the Americans and British were fighting, the Americans had to retreat up the Mississippi River to Fort Madison. The commanding officer, Lieutenant Hamilton, was able to save the fort for a time, but he was never sent more men or supplies.

The Indians, spurred on by the British, thought this would be a good time to renew their attack on the fort. As the soldiers waited week after week for supplies that never came, the Indians prowled around. No soldier dared show his head above the walls.

By September, Lieutenant Hamilton knew that they would have to outwit the Indians if they were to be saved. He called his men together.

"Men, we have waited as long as we can for supplies," he said to them. "We will have to save ourselves."

"There is no way out of here, sir." One of the men

voiced the fear they all felt. "Sooner or later we must give ourselves up to the Indians."

"Nonsense," spoke up the lieutenant. "I think we have a chance. It may not work, but it is better than waiting to be killed." As he spoke he walked to the window and pointed to the river. "We will dig a trench to the river. If we work on our hands and knees, I'm sure we can do it without being seen. Do you want to chance it?"

Every hand went up. Anything was better than waiting to be tomahawked by Black Hawk's band.

The soldiers began digging the trench. The Indians continued to prowl around the fort, shooting burning arrows, but they did not observe the men at work on the trench. Night and day they worked feverishly to complete the digging. Finally it was finished. One by one, under cover of night, they slipped out the trench to the river. The last man set fire to the fort as he left.

Before the Indians realized what had happened, the fort was in flames and the soldiers were safe in boats on the Mississippi. All that was left of the fort was a chimney standing as a grim reminder of the warfare between the Indians and the American soldiers.

The War of 1812 ended in January of 1815. When Black Hawk was told that peace had been made, he wept. He had wanted the British to win. But he still had many scores to settle with the Americans. During the war he had returned to Saukenuk to find that American soldiers had raided his village. During the skirmish, his young son had been killed.

The Black Hawk War

By 1827, the white settlers had begun to push into the area around Saukenuk, and in 1829 they took possession of the village while the Indians were gone to their winter hunting grounds. The treaty had stated that the Indians could stay on the land until the white settlers wanted to take it over. Now the Indians were told that they must leave by April 30, 1830. Anyone who stayed would be forcibly removed. President Andrew Jackson signed the order, saying, "If I remember aright, this Indian chief, Black Hawk, and his band fought against us in the late war. Am I correct?"

Black Hawk refused to go, even when he was told that the Government would force him and his band to leave the village. General Gaines told him to move to the west side of the river within two days or the soldiers would move him. Black Hawk was still there at the end of two days. When a volunteer group arrived to remove the old war chief, they found the village deserted. Under cover of a storm, the Indians had crossed over to the Iowa side.

The following year Black Hawk made one last attempt to return to his beloved Saukenuk. As he brooded over how he had been wronged, he heard the Indian women weeping for their lost homes. He heard the children crying from hunger, for there had been no crops that year. He thought of the murder of his son. The young braves were clamoring for war. Black Hawk was mistakenly told at this time that the British would come to his aid if he went to war again against the Americans and that the land would once again be restored to him.

In April, 1832, Black Hawk and his warriors, along with the women and children, crossed over to the Illinois side of the river in defiance of the terms of the treaty. The general of the United States Army sent a message ordering him back to the other side, but Black Hawk refused. The militia was called out to help the army regulars. In the War* that followed, Black Hawk was hopelessly outnumbered. Prepared to defend his people as long as he could, he fought under tremendous disadvantage to gain time for the women and children to get back across the river.

The army disregarded Black Hawk's signal of surrender, and the Indians—warriors, women, and children —were brutally shot down in the rout. Black Hawk was captured. The old war chief was forced to bow his proud head to the superior numbers and weapons of the white man.

The army sent the Indian chief to a prison in St. Louis. Later he was moved to a prison in Virginia. In 1833 he was taken to Washington to meet President Andrew Jackson, who arranged for his release. Black Hawk returned again to his beloved land along the Mississippi.

The Death of Black Hawk

After the Black Hawk War, the relentless push of the white settlers shifted the Indian frontier to Iowa. Iowa was Black Hawk's last home. He built a home on the banks of the Des Moines River near Fort Madison. Here he spent his remaining days watching the river slip along toward the place where it joined his cherished river, the Mississippi.

In October of 1838, Black Hawk died. Even in death the old war chief was not to find peace. During his life time the white man took his land, and when he was dead, they robbed his grave. His body was dug up and plans were made to exhibit the skull. Friends of Black Hawk appealed to Territorial Governor Robert Lucas for help in finding the bones. They had been taken to Illinois. Governor Lucas demanded their return, and

---

* This is called the Black Hawk War.

Iowans remember Black Hawk. Black Hawk Lake in Sac County.

they were placed in a historical collection in Burlington. When the museum burned in 1855, the bones became ashes. The tragedy of his life followed Black Hawk even in death.

The people of Iowa keep the memory of this proud chief alive by calling themselves Hawkeyes. In March, 1838, the editor of the Fort Madison Patriot suggested the name as a way of remembering the old chief. There was never an official adoption, but Iowans liked the name. Iowa became known as the Hawkeye State, and Iowans today refer to themselves as Hawkeyes.

Chapter 10

THE WATCHFUL FOX

Keokuk, the Watchful Fox, was born in the Sac village of Saukenuk in 1780. When he was very young, he learned that he could sway the opinions of others by his speeches. He developed this ability until he became a great orator. Black Hawk said he had a "smooth tongue". Although he was considered a great warrior, it was his ability to influence people with his speech that eventually won him the position of chief of the Sac and Fox.

His chance to become a chief came when Black Hawk left the village to go to war on the side of the British in the War of 1812.

A tribal council had been called.

"The white man is coming to destroy our village," one of the council announced.

"We must leave our village," said one of the old men sadly. "White men have horses and guns and will kill us all. We must save our women and children before it is too late. We can cross the Great River and be safe on the other side."

Nodding their heads in agreement, the old men of the council began to make plans to move.

"Do not forsake our village," Keokuk pleaded. "Our home is here. Let us stay and defend it."

"Black Hawk is gone," answered the tribesmen. "We have no one to lead us in war. We must cross the river."

"I will lead you," answered Keokuk, shrewdly. "If you make me a war chief, I will defend our homes and our women and children. The white man will not destroy our village if I am your leader."

His willingness to place himself in a position of danger won him the admiration of the tribal council.

Keokuk was made a war chief by his tribe, but he did not have to defend the village. The rumor that the village was to be destroyed was false. Nevertheless, when Black Hawk returned from the War, he found many of his tribesmen following Keokuk.

The Beginning of the Rivalry Between Black Hawk and Keokuk

By 1827 the white settlers were pushing into the area around Saukenuk. The order from the Government came in 1830 for the Indians to move to the Iowa side of the river. Keokuk saw a good chance of becoming the leading spokesman for his tribe if he peaceably obeyed the orders of the Government.

A bitter quarrel broke out between Black Hawk and Keokuk.

"You are willing to give up our home and the home of our ancestors," said Black Hawk. "You have sent a crier through our village saying it is the wish of the

111

Great Father that we should move to the west side of the Mississippi."

"You know that we must move," reasoned Keokuk. "Surely it is better to build our new village on the Iowa River now before we start on the winter's hunt. Then the village will be ready for our people when we return in the spring."

"Go build your village," Black Hawk said scornfully. "When I return in the spring, I will come to Saukenuk."

The following spring, Keokuk and his followers built their new village on the banks of the Iowa River. Black Hawk looked with contempt at the members of the tribe who were following the leadership of Keokuk. Black Hawk and his group went back to Saukenuk. Much of it had been destroyed. They set about rebuilding the village.

"Plant corn as usual," he told the squaws. "And if white man comes," he continued to the braves, "we will tell them to leave. We will not kill any of their cattle or destroy any of their property, but we will defend our land. This land is ours."

One day Keokuk visited the village.

"Why have you come?" demanded Black Hawk.

"I have come to see if you will bring your people to the new village on the Iowa River. We have built many lodges and there is room for us all."

Black Hawk knew that Keokuk was trying to get control of the entire tribe.

"Go!" Black Hawk declared angrily. "There is no friendship between us. You are a coward to abandon our village to strangers."

Keokuk returned to the Iowa side of the river. He knew Black Hawk was playing a losing game. The time would soon come, he felt sure, when he alone would be

112

recognized as the head chief. The order came from the Government for the Indians to be moved out. Under threat of force, Black Hawk moved his band across the river. They built a village a short way up the Iowa River from the village of Keokuk.

Keokuk and Black Hawk continued to be rivals. Black Hawk felt that Keokuk had sold out to the enemy. He had nothing but contempt for a man who would give in to the demands of the white man. When Keokuk heard of Black Hawk's plans to go to war, he again tried to advise him.

"There are a thousand American soldiers to every one of your braves," he told Black Hawk. "If you go back across the river, every one of you will be killed."

Black Hawk's Attempt To Get Followers

Black Hawk's answer was to come to Keokuk's village to persuade some of Keokuk's braves to join him.

He set up a war post just outside of the door of Keokuk's lodge. He drove his tomahawk into the post. All the Indians recognized this as a declaration of war.

Slowly but defiantly, Black Hawk and his braves started a war dance around the post. The dance was accompanied by war whoops and war songs. The dance became faster, the war whoops louder. Keokuk watched as one by one his braves became hypnotized by the fury of the war dance and joined in the ceremony around the war post.

Louder and louder the chants echoed up and down the river and across the wooded hills. At the height of the frenzy, Black Hawk dramatically raised his arms and signalled for silence.

"We have suffered many wrongs at the hands of the white man," he began. "They have brought their fire water to our village, made wolves out of our braves and warriors, compelled us to flee across the Mississippi, and then they have burned down our ancient village and run their plows through our graveyards. Let us be united again as a nation and at once cross the Mississippi. Let us rekindle our watch-fire under our ancient watch tower. When we recross the Mississippi, the British father will send us soldiers to fight our battles for us."

War hysteria filled the camp.

Keokuk Breaks the Spell

Keokuk broke through the circle and made his way to the war post. His braves were under the spell of Black Hawk, clamoring for war. He chose his words carefully.

"I have heard and considered your demand to be led forth upon the warpath against the palefaces," he said calmly. "Their cabins are as plentiful as the trees in the forest, and their soldiers are springing up like the grass on the prairies. All we can reasonably expect is to wreak our vengeance upon their hated heads and fall. There are too many of them. Any thought of overcoming them is hopeless."

The spell cast by the war dance had begun to wear off. Some of the braves were beginning to weaken in their determination to go to war. Keokuk could sense this and he continued.

"It is my duty as your chief to be your father while in the paths of peace, and your leader while on the war path. But what shall we do with our women and children? We dare not leave them behind."

The braves were looking at each other. What Keokuk was saying was true. There were many things they had not considered.

114

"I will lead you forth upon the warpath," Keokuk continued, "but upon this condition: that we first put our wives and children, our aged and infirm, gently to sleep in that slumber which knows no waking this side of spirit land. We cannot take them with us and we dare not leave them behind us."

The spell was broken. One by one Keokuk's warriors returned to him. Keokuk knew he had done a good job of persuading when he saw many of Black Hawk's followers coming along with them.

Black Hawk was defeated in his purpose, but he was not to be deterred. The next morning he proceeded down the Iowa River to make his tragic journey across the Mississippi.

In the Black Hawk War that followed, Black Hawk was captured and made a prisoner. When he was released, he was told he could make his home in Iowa, but he could never again be a chief. Keokuk was given the honor of being chief of the Sac and Fox because the Government said he was a "peaceful man". This was his reward for not making war on the whites.

Black Hawk was magnificent in his devotion to a hopeless cause. Keokuk was a man who desired peace, perhaps peace at too high a price. Black Hawk chose to go down to glorious defeat rather than to sacrifice what he felt to be right. Keokuk was willing to compromise. To the end of his life, Black Hawk remained a proud Indian. Devoted to his family, he never gave in to the vices of the white man that befell many of his fellow Indians. Keokuk, on the other hand, became addicted to the use of liquor and died an alcoholic. Through these two men the triumph and the tragedy of the Indian story is told.

Chapter 11

INKPADUTA AND THE
SCARLET BAND

When the United States Government stepped in to stop the quarrels between the Sac and Fox and the Sioux Indians in 1830, they established a line between them extending from the mouth of the Upper Iowa River to the Des Moines River. The Sioux on the north donated 20 miles to the strip, and the Sac and Fox on the south donated 20 miles. The strip became known as the Neutral Ground and became the property of the United States Government. The rules governing this Neutral Strip allowed all tribes to hunt on the land, but would not allow any tribe to attack another.

All of the tribes obeyed the order with the exception of a small tribe within the Sioux led by Wamdisapa. Again and again Wamdisapa crossed over the line and led his tribe against the Sac and Fox until the Sioux council finally outlawed the warlike tribe.

When Wamdisapa died, his son, Sidominadota, became chief of the outlaw tribe. He continued the warlike attacks against the other tribes and sometimes even against his own Sioux tribesmen who tried to stop him.

Henry Lott, The Outlaw Trader

Among the early settlers who were just beginning to come into this western part of the state was an outlaw white trader named Henry Lott. He and his band of desperadoes sold whiskey to the Indians and stole from both the white and red men. One day he robbed Sidominadota of a string of ponies, and Sidominadota chased him out of the country.

Some time later, Lott returned to Iowa and again encountered Sidominadota in Humboldt County. Lott vowed to get even with the Sioux chief. On the pretense of taking Sidominadota out on an elk hunt, Lott and his son waylaid the Indian and murdered him. Then, disguised as Indians, the two white men went back to Sidominadota's lodge and killed the chief's wife, mother, and all but two of his children, a boy and a girl. These two escaped to carry the news of the tragedy to Sidominadota's brother, Inkpaduta, known as Scarlet Point. Inkpaduta now became chief of the tribe, and Lott hurriedly left Iowa for California. Inkpaduta continued to war against his own Sioux tribe as had his father and brother, but now he had added another enemy—the white men as he knew them through Henry Lott.

Iowa in 1856

By 1856 a few settlers had moved into northwest Iowa. Arriving just before winter set in, they hastily built cabins along the Little Sioux River. Another small settlement had started near the Okoboji lake region. These settlements were outposts of the white men's civil-

117

ization. Fort Dodge, some eighty miles away, was the nearest place where men could go for provisions.

The winter was long and cold. Provisions began to run low. Some families survived on corn bread and molasses.

While the settlers in the cabins did manage to keep warm, the Indians in their skin tepees were not faring so well. Wandering bands of Sioux came to the cabins in increasing numbers for food and warmth. Sometimes it was hard to get them to leave the fire after they had greedily eaten the corn bread, but to the white settlers they seemed harmless.

Inkpaduta at Smithland

In the winter of 1856, Inkpaduta and his straggling band of outlaws, called the Scarlet Band, were wintering on the Adams farm by the Little Sioux River. This spot was near the little settlement of Smithland in what is now Woodbury County. The warriors of the band spent the winter hunting along the river while the women traded their beadwork to the white settlers for food and clothing. The entire group camped in nine tepees.

Mr. James Adams, who was a boy on the Adams farm, recalled, "The Indians were quiet and sociable all winter." He remembered that there were about 35 Indians in all and that about 15 were warriors. Inkpaduta's family consisted of his wife and four sons.

"Inkapaduta wasn't near as sociable as the younger ones," this pioneer commented. "He was offish and sullen and kept to himself. He was a little under six feet tall, heavy set and powerful and in the neighborhood of 60 years old. His face was horribly pock-marked and his hair was red. The other Indians, with two exceptions, were all taller than I."

118

The white men had brought many diseases into the new frontiers, particularly small pox. Thousands of Indians died from the epidemics which spread rapidly, first through the villages of the Algonquin and later to the more isolated Sioux tribes. Inkpaduta had been a victim of small pox, and the disease had left deep scars on his face.

As the winter became more severe and food became scarce, the people of Smithland suspected the Scarlet Band of robbing their corn supply. In an effort to drive the Indians away, the men at Smithland took the guns away from the Indians and told them that they would not return them until Inkpaduta had agreed to move his band on down the Missouri River. Inkpaduta, fearing the strength of the white settlers, moved on without redeeming his guns, but not south, as the settlers thought, but north.

The Scarlet Band Moves Up the Little Sioux

Moving up the Little Sioux River as the winter snows began to fill the valleys, the warriors of the Scarlet Band marveled at the number of cabins that had sprung up since their trip downstream in the late summer. The cabins were all alike, made of logs with heavy puncheon[1] doors hung on wooden hinges. Inside, the dirt floor was leveled and covered with prairie hay and a rag carpet, which Inkpaduta's warriors had found made fine blankets.

Just north of Cherokee, Inkapaduta saw a sleek herd of cattle and some fat pigs near the Milford colony. Flying Cloud and Roaring Cloud, Inkpaduta's twin sons, pushed their way into the cabin in search of food. Inkpaduta and the remaining braves shot the livestock. The

---

[1] Puncheon—split logs with the face roughly smoothed.

119

The Kirchner cabin at Peterson

women set to work at once skinning the animals, cutting up the meat, and loading it on their sled-like travois. A whoop of glee drew Inkpaduta's attention to the cabin. A cloud of feathers billowed from the door. The twins had found the white man's feather ticks and were ripping the mattresses apart and scattering the feathers in the wind.

The little band of Indians continued on up the Little Sioux Valley. Near Peterson, Inkpaduta noted with displeasure another new cabin across the river from the Kirchner cabin. He had visited this settlement last summer. He remembered the visit well. Kirchner had two strong sons, Gust and Jake, just about the age of his twin sons. What fun the sons had had with the two white boys, wrestling in the summer sun and shooting at acorns set up in the fork of a tree! Inkpaduta looked

120

over his Band. He selected six young warriors, nodded to his twin sons, and led them across the snow to the Kirchner cabin. There would be food here, he knew, for the Kirchners had been kind to them before.

Jane Bicknell and Inkpaduta

The snow had nearly covered the tiny cabins of the Kirchner and Bicknell families on the banks of the Little Sioux near Peterson. The winter had been severe, but a brief warming spell had begun to settle down over the little valley. Yesterday a messenger had come up river to warn the two families that "The Indians are to Mr. Waterman's."

Twenty people were crowded into the Kirchner cabin that Sunday morning in February as the nine Indians came up the bank. For 24 hours the settlers had waited in the cabin, singing hymns to keep up their courage. Now the Indians were approaching. Young Gust, peering through the window, recognized his Indian playmates of the past summer. He opened the door and stepped out to meet the visitors. The family dog ran out of the cabin, barking at the hideously painted Indians. There was a shot.

"They've shot Gust!" gasped Jake, the younger brother. The frantic settlers waited breathlessly in the cabin. The door swung open, and there was Gust, calmly ushering in the nine Indians and welcoming them as if they were old friends. Outside the pet dog lay dead in the snow.

Jane Bicknell, a young school girl, tells in her diary of Inkpaduta's visit to the Kirchner cabin.

"Inkpaduta was one of the most hideous things I'd ever seen in my life. The Indians came and searched our house. Took all the flour and Indian meal we had.

121

When they began to take the last of the flour, Mrs. Kirchner stopped them. 'That's for *my* papooses!' And they didn't take it."

Mrs. Kirchner remained calm, sitting in her rocking chair with her small children about her. The children's pet kitten—probably the one and only kitten on the western Iowa frontier—mewed loudly. Mrs. Kirchner, hoping to save the kitten from a fate similar to that of the pet dog, quickly slipped the kitten under her apron and continued rocking quietly back and forth. Luckily everyone had turned just then to see another warrior enter the cabin. He was carrying a chunk of frozen carcass that he had cut from one of the Kirchner oxen that had died several days ago. The warrior made signs to Mrs. Kirchner to cook the meat. She rose, cradling the kitten under her apron, and without being seen, tucked the tiny kitten under the pillow on the bed.

After the Indians had eaten, they searched the cabin. One warrior pounced upon Gust's best gun and ran from the cabin. Taking all the food they could find, they went outside. They picked up the body of the dead dog and the rest of the oxen meat and departed. But they did not take the kitten. The little pet had slept peacefully under the pillow all during the unwelcome visit of the Indians.

Jane continues in her diary: "The Indians left. Mary and I started to come over to our house to see what the Indians had done. Saw some more Indians coming down the hill so we went back. Jake and Gust skinned the cattle the Indians had killed."

"February 18: Gust and Jake went up to Mr. Mead's. The Indians took Harriet Mead down to their tents and made her stay all night. They threw knives at Gust and put their guns at his breast and said they would shoot him."

"February 20: We moved home from Mr. Kirchner's. We found our partition torn down. The tea-kettle, frying pan, Mother's little wheel and the carpet were gone."

"February 22: Sunday: Jake is here and I have not much chance to write. I have to listen to stories about the Indians. Jake says the Indians have killed all of Mr. Frinke's cattle, took everything they had in their home, emptied their feather beds, broke out the windows and did not leave a thing. Took five horses of Mr. Wilcoxes."

Inkpaduta Moves On Up the Little Sioux

With the provisions taken from the Kirchner and Mead cabins, Inkpaduta set up camp along the protected river bottom near Gillett Grove. Here for a time the Band enjoyed good days, food for all, and shelter at night. One day a messenger came running across the snow. One of Inkpaduta's warriors had been shot by a white man. Inkpaduta helped lift the lifeless body down from the tree where the white settlers had concealed it. The white men had fled. Inkpaduta, enraged, ordered his band to destroy the settlement. The warriors rushed to their work of destruction, killing the cattle and burning the Gillett cabins.

Then Inkpaduta and his band headed toward his favorite hunting grounds in the region of Lake Okoboji and Spirit Lake. The women could cut a hole in the ice and catch fish. There might be a fowl or two. There would be only one or two white cabins in that region.

Not only was the area a favorite hunting ground, but it was also sacred ground to all Sioux. The Indians believed that the Great Spirit moved mysteriously over the large body of water, sometimes troubling the water, sometimes making the lake peaceful.

The Scarlet Band reached the lake region on a cold,

clear Sunday morning in March. Inkpaduta stood on the east shore of Okoboji. Across the lake a thin wisp of smoke rose from a lone cabin. His eye swept across the lake. Another cabin! And yet another! He turned and scanned the horizon. White men! They were taking the sacred ground of his people. He strode down to his waiting warriors. He knew what he must do. The white men had gone too far!

The Spirit Lake Massacre

Breakfast was to be early that Sunday morning in the Gardner cabin, for Father and Mary's young husband, Harvey Luce, were going to start out on foot for Fort Dodge to secure enough provisions to last the winter. Fourteen-year old Abbie was stirring the mush kettle at the fireplace. The cabin door swung open. An Indian armed with a double-barrelled shotgun, cocked and loaded with ball, stood at the door.

At her mother's sharp cry, Abbie set another bowl on the table and ladled the hot mush into it. The Indian sat down. Soon the one room cabin was filled with other Indians, the huge Inkpaduta among them, greedily demanding food.

Into the middle of this confusion came Dr. Harriot and Bertell Snyder, neighbors of the Gardners. The two men had walked over to the Gardner cabin from their cabin on the opposite shore to give Mr. Gardner some letters that they wanted mailed in Fort Dodge. The Indians were now beginning to leave the cabin and roam around the little clearing. The white men held a hasty conference behind the cabin door. Mr. Gardner wanted to gather all the settlers of the lake region in his cabin, nearly 40 in all, and defend themselves. Snyder and Harriot thought this might anger the Indians.

124

The Indians were now driving off the Gardner cattle, shooting them down one by one as they scrambled through the snow drifts. Harriot and Snyder watched them go, and then circled through the oak grove to warn the other settlers.

The Gardners barred the cabin door and huddled inside. Two shots interrupted the silence. The Indians had shot Snyder and Dr. Harriot before they could warn the other settlers.

All day the Gardner family waited in the cabin, watching through the frost-covered windows. As the sun set behind the far shore of the lake, Rowland Gardner cautiously opened the door and stepped outside. Darting from tree to tree, he peered up the lake shore. Nine Indians, led by the huge Inkpaduta, were tramping through the deep snow toward the Gardner cabin.

"They're coming back!" Mr. Gardner shouted as he ran inside. "We'll have to fight them off ourselves."

Mrs. Gardner, cradling one of her tiny grandsons in her arms begged, "Don't provoke them, Rowland. Let's try being friendly. It worked this morning."

Against his better judgment, Mr. Gardner opened the door and admitted the Indians.

"Flour," one warrior demanded.

Mr. Gardner turned to the flour barrel. There was only a scraping left in the bottom. He bent over. A shot rang out. Mr. Gardner slumped over the barrel. The other Indians burst into a wild war whoop. One burly warrior seized Mother Gardner, another Mary. They dragged the women out the door and threw them down in the snow. As they lay helpless, the Indians beat them with the butts of their guns.

The massacre had begun!

Young Abbie had been huddling in the corner of the

cabin trying to protect the little Luce children and her younger brother. The Indians next pounced upon the children and killed them. But instead of turning upon Abbie as their next victim, they broke into a wild dance, breaking open trunks, tearing up clothes, and ripping apart beds.

For six days the enraged Scarlet Band, smeared in the black war paint of the Sioux, murdered and plundered the entire settlement, killing 43 settlers. They carried off four women as prisoners: young Abbie Gardner, Mrs. William Marble, Mrs. Noble, and Mrs. Thatcher.

Charles E. Flandrau, an Indian agent in charge of the Sioux at the time of the massacre, wrote in his report concerning the lake settlement: "It was the extreme outpost of civilization. A long and weary distance separated them from the most advanced settlement in Iowa. To the west and northwest of them lay the limitless plains extending to the Rocky Mountains, inhabited only by the Indian and the buffalo. To the north the nearest habitations were on the upper waters of the Minnesota River, a distance of nearly a hundred miles over a primitive wilderness, and the nearest possible point from which protection could have been looked for was Fort Ridgley[1], a US post on a Sioux reservation, two days' journey by horse in fair weather."

Kidnapped by the Scarlet Band

Northwest into Minnesota beyond the Pipestone quarries, Inkpaduta led his band. During the long marches the three women and the young girl were forced to carry the heavy packs through the deep snow. They were often hungry and sick and always cold. Mrs. Thatcher grew

[1] Fort Ridgely was on the Minnesota River near the present town of New Ulm.

ill. When she became so weak she could no longer keep up the march, the Indians became disgusted. As they were crossing the Big Sioux River, they pushed her off the log crossing and left her to drown in the icy waters.

In the meantime, a white settler, Morris Markham, coming to visit in the lake settlement, came upon the empty cabins. He hurried back to Fort Dodge with the news of the tragedy. Many years earlier the United States Government had stationed dragoons, who were mounted soldiers, in various forts across the frontier to protect the white settlers from Indian attacks. But later the authorities had felt that there was no longer any danger from Indians in Iowa and had ordered the company of dragoons stationed at Fort Dodge to abandon the fort. Since there were no dragoons, 80 citizens formed a posse and started out across the blizzard-swept prairie.

Charles Flandreau, the Indian agent, tells of his first news of the massacre: "The first news of the massacre reached me on the 18th of March, some ten days after its occurence. Two young men brought me a statement of the facts. These boys traveled the whole distance on foot, through snow, thirty inches deep and were nearly exhausted when they reached my agency. I immediately consulted with Colonel Alexander of the 10th US Infantry at Fort Ridgely and made a requisition for troops. The difficulty that stared us in the face was the certainty that any hostile movement against Inkpaduta would result in the slaughter of the captives. I was planning a rescue through negotiation and ransom."

Abbie is Rescued

As spring came on, the Scarlet Band settled down far into the Dakota Territory. One day two strange Indians walked into camp and offered to buy the prisoners. For a gun, a blanket, and a few trinkets, Inkpaduta sold Mrs. Marble to the strangers. Little did Inkpaduta know that they were the Indians sent out by the Indian agent, Flandreau. The wily old chief would sell only one of the captives, but the two Indians promised that they would return for Abbie and Mrs. Noble.

Life was easier now for the two remaining captives. There were no more long marches. The women were even allowed to share the same tepee. One evening Roaring Cloud, Inkpaduta's son, entered the tepee and ordered Mrs. Noble to get out. She refused. In a fit of anger, he seized his tomahawk and killed her. Only the fourteen-year old Abbie was left.

It was June before the two Indians returned to bargain for the captive girl. Inkpaduta finally consented to release Abbie in exchange for 12 blankets, 2 kegs of powder, 20 pounds of tobacco, 32 yards of squaw cloth, 37½ yards of calico, and an assortment of trinkets.

The kidnapped girl was free.

The friendly Indians hurried Abbie off to where they had hidden a team and wagon. With Abbie driving the team and the Indians leading the way, they started the long journey back to civilization. Twenty days later, Abbie arrived in St. Paul and was presented to Governor Medary. The governor wanted to adopt Abbie, but she wanted to return to her one remaining sister, who had been away visiting at the time of the massacre. On the 5th of July, Abbie was finally reunited with her sister, Eliza, in Hampton.

Many years later Abbie Gardner returned to the Gardner cabin at Okoboji. She purchased the cabin, remodeled it, and made it her home for the rest of her life. She wrote a book about her experience called *The*

The scene of the Spirit Lake Indian Massacre at Lake Okoboji

History of the Spirit Lake Massacre and the Captivity of Miss Abbie Gardner.

The State of Iowa erected a tall, needle-like monument just in front of the Gardner cabin in memory of the white settlers. The cabin and monument can be seen today bordering Lake Okoboji.

And Inkpaduta?

For a quarter of a century the name of Inkpaduta struck terror in the hearts of whites and Indians alike

129

in the northwestern part of Iowa. But the Spirit Lake Massacre cannot be considered an isolated event. The Massacre touched off a chain of events that eventually had national significance.

In 1862, Inkpaduta joined his other Sioux tribesmen in the uprising in Minnesota near New Ulm and finally climaxed his lawless career in 1876 at the Battle of Little Big Horn, where he helped engineer the ambush of General Custer and his men. Custer's last stand was the greatest defeat that the white man ever suffered against the red man. According to Sioux tradition, Custer was killed "by fire belched forth from a Winchester" held by Inkpaduta's son, Thunder Cloud.

The immediate causes of the Iowa Massacre were the lack of food during the severe winter of 1856-1857 and the unfriendly treatment the Scarlet Band received at Smithland and Gillett Grove. But underlying these were deeper reasons that set off future Sioux trouble: the resentment at the white man's invasion of Sioux territory, the bitterness the Sioux felt toward the lawless whites such as Lott, and the contempt they felt toward the tricks and treaties of the white men.

Like Black Hawk, Inkpaduta rebelled—not in the same stately way—but in the only way he understood: as an outlaw. In Inkpaduta can be seen the degrading of the Indian character through certain elements of the white man's culture. As one early Iowa editor commented: "Many rude and even wicked things take place in the early settlement of a new country, and many rude and unrefined persons find their way first among the wilds of the west..." Henry Lott and Inkpaduta represent the worst of both the red and white cultures, and many innocent people had to suffer because of them.

The Indians never again molested the white settlers

of Iowa. As Kettle Chief's agreement with Dubuque marked the first Indian concession to the demands of the white man, so the Spirit Lake Massacre marked the end of the red man's struggle to keep his Iowa.

As for Inkpaduta ... he fled with Sitting Bull to Canada, where he died an old man, completely blind.

Chapter 12

MESQUAKIES OF MESQUAKIA

When Iowa grain fields wave golden in the August sun, and corn tassels feather into yellow-green plumes, the Mesquakie Indians assemble on the Old Battleground for their annual Pow-Wow. Here along the Iowa River near Tama the remnants of the once great tribe of Sac and Fox Indians relive their history in song and dance.

At any other time of year the Old Battleground is still, and the Mesquakies live a life quite similar to that of their white neighbors. The nearly 700 Mesquakie Indians live on the 3,600 acre tract which is owned by the Mesquakie tribe, in houses like the well-known white frame house of the Iowa farmer.

The Mesquakie children attend grade school on the settlement. They dress in the manner of all school children: T-shirts, blue jeans, skirts and blouses. They study from the same textbooks as all Iowa school children. When they leave their Indian grade school, they attend junior and senior high school in the neighboring town of

Tama. Often they continue their education in the universities and colleges of Iowa.

But every August the clock is turned back, and the Mesquakies don their colorful costumes with the beaded ornaments and the sweeping headdress of feathers and bring to modern Iowa a glimpse of their proud past. But the history of the Mesquakie tribe is a story of sadness.

Forced To Leave Iowa

The Mesquakies were Woodland Indians that at one time had lived as far north as the St. Lawrence River. Pushed westward by other tribes of Indians as well as by the white men, they lived for many years along the Mississippi River. When their tribe became small, the Fox or Reynards, as the French traders called them, joined with their relatives the Sac, who were similar in customs and religion. Although the two tribes lived together for many years as one people and the United States Government dealt with them as one tribe, the Mesquakies kept their own tribal customs among themselves.

When President Thomas Jefferson purchased the Louisiana Territory, the Fox, or Mesquakies, had three villages in this area: one north of the rapids of Rock River in Illinois, one 12 miles beyond Dubuque's lead mines, and one on the Turkey River. Little by little the Indians of Iowa had been forced to give up their hunting grounds until in 1845 the last of the Mesquakies were escorted by the dragoons to the Brown County Indian Reservation across the Missouri River in Kansas.

The white men who crowded into Iowa upon the heels of the departing Indians soon found that the dragoons had not rounded up all the Mesquakies. Some had hidden that October morning along the Iowa River.

133

Since the Mesquakies are by nature a gentle, peace-loving people, the white settlers left them alone to wander their old haunts.

The bare plains of the Kansas reservation did not seem like home to the rest of the little Mesquakie tribe. They were used to roaming over the gently rolling hills of the Iowa River Valley and seeking out the peaceful shady nooks that bordered the river. Furthermore, the Indian agent at the Kansas reservation insisted upon teaching the Indians some of the facts of the white man's civilization such as wearing clothes, living in houses, and raising livestock. These things did not interest the Mesquakie, and, characteristically, he ignored the instruction. The Kansas climate was different too, and many of the Indian children became ill.

"In Iowa, winters were never too cold, and the summers were always pleasant," commented one homesick Mesquakie.

The Mesquakies Return

One day the governor of Iowa, James Grimes, looked up from his office desk in the Old State Capitol at Iowa City to see a Mesquakie chief and two warriors standing before him.

The chief, Mamanwanika, drew a bag of money from his blanket and threw it on the desk.

"Count," he ordered.

The Governor emptied the bag and counted out the silver.

"$730," said the puzzled Governor.

The Mesquakie continued, "White man counts $730. Indians count $730."

"But what do you want me to do with the money?" inquired the Governor.

134

"We want to buy land," replied the chief.

"But you have your reservation in Kansas," the Governor countered.

"White man buys land, white man's business. Indian buys land, Indian's business," stated the chief firmly.

Governor Grimes knew that the Mesquakies were not happy on their Kansas reservation. No doubt the $730 had been carefully saved from the yearly payment given by the United States Government to each Indian who lived on a reservation.

Governor Grimes promised the Indians that he would see what he could do about buying some land for them. Indians at this time were not considered citizens of the United States and could not own land. Governor Grimes purchased 80 acres of land bordering the Iowa River for the Mesquakies in his own name.

When news of this purchase reached the Mesquakies in Kansas, they sold their ponies to buy more land and walked the many miles back to their beloved Iowa. So happy were they to return that the warriors fell down and kissed the ground. They even carried back their dead and buried them on the bluffs of the Iowa River.

Troubles in Mesquakia

Those first winters were difficult for the new Indian settlement, for they had no supply of food laid aside. Through the kindness of the white settlers, particularly the members of the Amana colonies, the Mesquakies survived. More land was purchased until the settlement stretched to over 3,600 acres. Pushetonika, a nephew of the famous Chief Poweshiek for whom Poweshiek County was named, became the chief.

As tribal leader, Pushetonika taught his people the ancient customs, legends, stories, and rites of the tribe.

He taught them that life is one of the most sacred things to a true Mesquakie, that all living things are precious and a part of the Great Spirit, and that all people are partners together. A good Mesquakie was to make friends wherever he went, to say things that were true, and to lead a life of kindness and love.

As the white settlers surrounded the Mesquakie land, the Indians found it hard to adjust to their strange new neighbors. Whenever they went out to hunt, they came upon white men's homesteads. One day some Indian children went by a white man's school. The white children came out and threw rocks and sticks at the little copper-skinned children. The older Indians, seeing this, supposed that white people taught their children in their school houses to throw things at people.

"They teach things differently than Indians, and we don't want our children to be taught those things," said the chief.

When the Government set up schools on the Mesquakie settlement, it was no wonder that the tribal fathers, at first, refused to send their children to the school.

A United Presbyterian Mission Church was built near the edge of the settlement in 1893, but very few of the Mesquakies ever accepted Christianity.

Mesquakia Today

Chief Pushetonika died in 1919. Before his death he appointed a council of five to rule over the tribe. This is the type of government that the settlement has today.

The tribe once had 15 clans. Some of the older clans have died out but the Wolf, Bear, Thunder, Fox, Eagle, and Buffalo clans remain today. Each clan has its own songs, some of which have words, some just syllables.

It is important to a Mesquakie to be enrolled in the tribe

There are as many as 80 unwritten songs that are memorized and sung in a special order.

The Mesquakie language is taught to the children by their parents and is spoken in the home. The language changes from generation to generation, for the language has never been written down. Many of the children learn English for the first time when they enter school.

It is important to a Mesquakie to be enrolled in the tribe, since the lands are held in the name of the Mesquakie tribe. Tribal membership, which is limited to the Indian men only, is passed down from father to son.

Community life on the settlement consists of religious feasts, dancing, games, and family get-togethers. In

137

their small garden plots the Mesquakies still raise Indian corn, beans, squash, and pumpkins and often dry them in the same manner as did their ancestors. Wickiups can be seen at Pow-Wow time, and some of the families use them for summer kitchens.

The Mesquakies' Influence on Iowa

The charming words and legends of the Mesquakie language are woven into the heart and life of modern Iowa. The Wapsipinicon River, which flows through the lovely meadows of eastern Iowa into the Mississippi, is so named from a legend of a beautiful Indian maiden called Wapsi. According to the legend, Wapsi fell in love with Pinicon, a handsome son of an enemy chieftain. The young people would meet in secret on the beautiful river. One day, while canoeing on the river, Pinicon was shot by the arrow of one of Wapsi's tribesmen. She stood up to help the wounded Pinicon and upset the canoe. The two lovers were drowned. The river was named Wapsipinicon, and according to the legend their voices can be heard even today in the rippling of the waters of the Wapsipinicon.

The name of Maquoketa, a town in eastern Iowa, came from the Mesquakie. Bears were numerous in this region. When the Indians wanted to hunt for bear, they would go here, for the name means "bear here."

Nine Iowa counties are named from words of the Mesquakie language: *Appanoose*-an Indian chief, *Black Hawk*-the famous Sac chief, *Keokuk*-the Fox chief, *Muscatine*-a tribe of the Sac and Fox, *Poweshiek*-a Sac chief, *Sac*-Sac Indians, *Tama*-Fox Indian chief, Taimah, *Wapello*-Fox chief, *Pottawattamie*-Potawatomi tribe of the Sac and Fox.

Pow-Wow time at Tama

Pow-Wow Time

At Pow-Wow time at Mesquakia, one sees a united community working for the success of the famous Iowa festival. Everyone in the tribe has a part in its production whether it be dancing or selling souvenirs. At Pow-Wow time the Mesquakies relive the days of long ago and give the white man an insight into the culture of this one remaining Indian tribe in Iowa.

The Pow-Wow first started as a field day, but Chief Pushitonika changed it into a Pow-Wow. A plot of land, called the Old Battleground, is set aside for the event.

The Mesquakies say that in 1830 a band of Sioux Indians attacked them at this site while they were sleeping. The Sioux had silently surrounded them in the night, getting into position to attack by imitating owl and wolf calls. At dawn the Sioux attacked. The battle raged most of the morning. In the midst of the battle a Mesquakie maiden, a descendant of Chief Poweshiek, entered the fight and killed a Sioux warrior. For this deed she was awarded a skunk skin, a high honor for an

139

Indian woman, and became the only Mesquakie woman allowed to dance the war dance with the other warriors who had killed an enemy.

Through the songs and dances of the Pow-Wow, the Mesquakies tell of this battle, of the granting of the rights of the lead mines to Dubuque, and of incidents from the Black Hawk War. The dances are performed in bright Indian costumes. The men depict the theme of the dance while the women and young girls dance in groups around them in a slow, shuffling step. The tom-toms beat, and the bells jangle. To be selected the champion dancer of the Pow-Wow is an honor for any Mesquakie. The steps of the dance are not written down, but are memorized by the chief dancer. The dances include such titles as the Friendship Dance, the Eagle Dance, the Green Corn Dance, and the Bean Dance.

The settlement at Tama is unique in the history of the Indians of America. Mesquakia is not a reservation. The Indians own their own land, and they are very proud of this fact. They have a deep respect for their land. To them it is not just so many acres to be planted to corn for profit. To them the land is their home, a place to be loved, a place that will always be there for the Mesquakies. The Mesquakies rent out most of their land to their white neighbors and use the money to pay the taxes. Many of the men who live on the settlement work in industries in Marshalltown, Cedar Rapids, or Waterloo. Some of the Mesquakie women find work in Tama. But a Mesquakie often finds that he is a stranger outside Mesquakia. Even if he lives off the settlement, he feels his true home is Mesquakia.

This tiny area of Indian culture in the middle of Iowa's farms and industries still holds much of the charm and dignity of a proud people.

On the Frontier

As the pioneers continued their march westward to the Mississippi River, the new West had become increasingly important. By 1828 the Westerners had been able to make their influence felt in a presidential election. Andrew Jackson was born on the frontier and was the first President of the common people. He was President of the United States when the Black Hawk War came to an end in 1832 and Iowa was opened up for settlement.

Having won a reputation as an Indian fighter, he pushed a policy of removing all of the Indians in the east into the Great Plains region west of the Mississippi River. This was accomplished by 1840.

The development and settlement of the Mississippi Valley was then speeded up. Up to this time the river systems had been the main method of transportation. Now roads were being built. The main road to the West was the Cumberland Road, running from Cumberland, Maryland, to Vandalia, Illinois. The completion of the Erie Canal in 1825 made a direct route from the East to the Great Lakes. By flatboats, barges and covered wagon, the pioneers moved westward in a steady stream and settled the Mississippi Valley.

In the twenty year period between 1820 and 1830, the population of the United States almost doubled—it increased from 12,800,000 to 23,200,000. Part of this increase was due to the 2,000,000 immigrants coming to the United States. As this increased population began to filter westward, Iowa received her share of the increase. The population of Iowa was 43,112 in 1840. Only six years later the population was 102,388. To provide protection for the new Iowa settlers, the United States Government established military posts throughout the frontier and sent out mounted soldiers, called Dragoons, to police the territory.

Various groups came into Iowa. Many just passed through on their way to the California gold rush. Others were restless frontiersmen, who, feeling the lure of more adventure and wealth farther westward, stayed a few years and moved on. But many arrived in Iowa and, recognizing the wealth to be wrested from the rich prairie land, remained to establish the foundations of the growing new state.

Chapter 13

DRAGOONS—POLICEMEN
OF THE FRONTIER

"Your orders, sir."

The 26-year old lieutenant took the packet of papers. His orders had come through at last. He had been waiting for them ever since he had decided that night at the close of the War to stay and make a career of the US Army.

He broke the seal and unfolded the papers. "You are ordered to appear at Camp Missouri where you will assume command of a detachment of Dragoons."

Camp Missouri? That outpost way out on the Missouri River?

Lieutenant Stephen W. Kearney tucked the orders into his pocket and walked slowly across the parade grounds to the log barracks.

A company of Dragoons! What a change it would be from the confining life of the military fort. Kearney had joined the army during the War of 1812 and had been

143

thrown into the midst of the fighting at Queenston Heights. He had been wounded during the encounter and taken a prisoner. Since that time he had been stationed at the military post near St. Louis.

Wherever Camp Missouri was, the life of a Dragoon sounded exciting. He had heard tales of these mounted policemen. "Watchmen on the borders," someone had called them. He knew their duty was to keep peace on the borders by protecting the settlers from the Indians, to keep order among the outlaw white men who often followed the moving frontier, and to keep squatters from staking out claims on Indian land.

Young Kearney soon learned that Camp Missouri was the farthest western outpost of the army, located near the point where Lewis and Clark had held their council with the Indians several years before. He had not been stationed at his new post long before he received further orders that he was to lead a small group of his mounted soldiers up to Fort Snelling near St. Paul in Minnesota. Not only would the trip relieve the routine for his Dragoons, who were now restless after a long winter spent in the army barracks, but perhaps they would be able to find a more practical route between the two military posts.

March of 1820

With five officers, 15 mounted Dragoons, and led by an Indian with his squaw and papoose, Kearney crossed the Missouri River July 2, 1820, and started out across the unexplored territory of western Iowa. The group camped near the mouth of the Boyer River after the first day's march, only to be deluged during the night by torrential rains.

The next day they moved up the Boyer Valley and

camped near the present town of Logan. On the third day Kearney felt that his men had spent two days in long marches and that they deserved to rest and celebrate since it was July 4th. This was probably the first 4th of July celebration ever held in Iowa, and it was staged not far from the present town of Woodbine. The men were issued extra rations and toasted their country in mint juleps, according to Kearney's report.

Up the Boyer Valley, across the headwaters of the Soldier River marched the Dragoons, seeing large herds of elk and buffalo feeding on the prairies. One day they shot a buffalo and roasted it over their evening camp fire. The soldiers enjoyed the buffalo steaks, but the Indian squaw ate so much that she got sick.

The life of a Dragoon on the march was not always an easy life. There were long marches by day through the wild unknown land, hastily set up camps beside a tiny stream, and always the constant exposure to the weather and insects of the summer. Sometimes the mosquitoes were so numerous that the men were forced to wear nets over their heads for protection. To relieve the monotony there was always game to hunt: elk, buffalo, prairie chickens, and water fowl. Occasionally they would meet a small wandering band of Indians, but never did they see a white man across the unsettled expanses of the rich new land.

Leaving the Boyer Valley and turning north somewhere between Dow City and Denison, the Dragoons and their young commander traveled for nearly 60 miles without seeing a tree or grove to mar the sweep of the blowing prairie grass. Near Peterson in Clay County they turned eastward and followed the Little Sioux River Valley north to Sioux Rapids and then cut across to Emmetsburg in Palo Alto County. At the point near the

Kearney State Park at Five Island Lake at Emmetsburg

shore of Five Island Lake at Emmetsburg, where Kearney and his Dragoons camped that hot summer night in 1820, the State of Iowa has now established Kearney State Park to commemorate the visit of the Dragoons. Crossing the two forks of the Des Moines River, Kearney led his band up to Northwood and on into Minnesota.

Of this portion of the state, Kearney reported in his diary: ". . . lacks timber, surface water, and the rugged character of the hills make the region well-nigh impassable forever preventing it from supporting more than a thinly scattered population." His prediction was not to prove accurate, for today this section of northwest Iowa is noted for its rich farm land.

From Minnesota the Dragoons floated down the Mississippi River in a rowboat. They passed Pike's Peak, several Indian villages, Dubuque's lead mines, the lone chimney that marked the site of Fort Madison, and landed at Fort Edwards, just opposite the mouth of the Des Moines River. The march of 1820 had covered 400 miles by land across western and northern Iowa and over 300 miles by water down the eastern border of the state through land unexplored except by Indians and a few French traders.

By 1834 Kearney was promoted to Lieutenant Colonel and instructed to return to the Iowa country to select a site for a second fort in Iowaland. Kearney arrived in the fall and work was started on the fort just above the mouth of the Des Moines River. The site chosen was on land once occupied by Tesson's apple orchard; in fact, some of the trees still remained. The place was then called Cut Nose from an Indian chief. Today the town of Montrose, a contraction of Mount of Roses, is located here. As soon as the Colonel's house was completed, he moved in with his Negro house slave. This was perhaps the first and one of the very few instances of slavery in Iowa.

March of 1835

By early spring Kearney was ordered to proceed with his Dragoons to the village of Wabasha, the Sioux Indian chief whom Pike had visited several years before. On his return he was to inspect the juncture of the Raccoon River and the Des Moines River as a possible site for another fort.

The expedition of 1835 started out on June 7th with three companies of Dragoons under the command of Colonel Kearney and three officers: Captain Nathan Boone, Lieutenant Albert M. Lea, and Captain H. S. Tanner. The party consisted of 170 men and seven or eight Indians as guides. They made an impressive sight crossing the prairie with their five wagons of provisions drawn by mule teams and driving a herd of beef cattle which they intended to butcher for food along the way.

Nathan Boone of the 1835 expedition was the youngest son of the famed Daniel Boone. He had served for fifteen years under Kearney and had at one time been in Iowa surveying the forty-mile strip of land in northern Iowa known as the Neutral Strip. This land extended east from the right fork of the Des Moines River and had been purchased from the Sioux and the Sac and Fox tribes. The Government had moved the Winnebagoes into this land and declared it neutral to protect them from the two more hostile tribes.

Lieutenant Lea was a soldier and an engineer. He kept a diary of all his experiences on the expedition and eventually wrote a book on the new land, the first book ever to be published about Iowa. He did not know what to call this land, so he referred to it as the Iowa territory, taking the name from the Iowa River.

The Dragoons of 1835 followed the divide between the Des Moines and Skunk rivers, passing near Keokuk's village on the Des Moines and through the present town of Colfax. Veering northward they reached a river flowing into the Des Moines which the men named Boone in honor of their captain. Today a county and a town in Iowa honor the name of Nathan Boone.

Progress was often slow, only four miles a day, for much of the area was swamp. Other days the group marched as many as 26 miles. From the present site of Boone, the Dragoons headed northeast toward Wabasha's village near the Mississippi River in Minnesota. Kearney spent about two weeks with Wabasha and signed a treaty with the Sioux chief. On the return journey an Indian guide lost his way, and the men found themselves wandering around some Minnesota lake unable to find a passage through or around. A group of Indians returning from a hunt consented to lead them out. Kearney found that what they thought had been the Iowa River was the St. Peter River of Minnesota. They traveled south and west to the west fork of the Des Moines River in Palo Alto County and marched down the west side of the Des Moines River to its juncture with the Raccoon, the present site of the city of Des Moines.

Food supplies were running short. Kearney told Lea to take two men and inspect the proposed fort site. Lea, in a hollowed out cottonwood log and accompanied by an Indian guide, rowed down to a point which was later to become the second Fort Des Moines, and eventually the capital city of Iowa.

By August they were back at Keokuk's village, and a few days later they were back at Fort Des Moines at Montrose. They had suffered no casualties nor sickness, but as one of the Dragoons grumbled, "only the stupid lack of food."

The report of this expedition concerning Iowa was much more favorable. Lea wrote in his book, "This is a region of great natural beauty and fertility with abundant out-cropping of coal, gypsum, and building stone."

After this expedition Stephen Kearney left Iowa for the far west where he served for a time as governor of California and fought in the Mexican War.

Captain Allen and the Dragoons

Although Colonel Kearney did not recommend establishing a fort as Captain Lea had designated, the United States Government decided otherwise. Seven years later

Captain James Allen of the Dragoons was sent out to locate a military post at the Raccoon Forks of the Des Moines River. He left Fort Sanford, just west of Ft. Madison, and went up the river.

Early white settlers in Marion County were amazed one morning to hear the shrill whistle of a steamboat echoing up and down the river. It was the steamship *Agatha* with Captain Allen on board. He informed the settlers that he was on his way to establish a military post at the Raccoon Forks. The settlers were glad to learn of this, for now they would have protection from the many tribes of Indians who wandered through the area. The little stern-wheeler, *Agatha,* had difficulty navigating the last leg of the journey up to the mouth of the Raccoon. She was stranded on a sand bar. Her machinery broke down. Captain Allen did not arrive at the new fort site until a month later.

The tanned army captain, stepping off the *Agatha,* made a striking picture with his full beard, sharp eyes, polished brass buttons, and big pistol. Watching from a distance was a tall Indian chief hugging his colorful blankets about him. It was Keokuk. The old Sac and Fox chief watched sadly as he realized that the white men were again thrusting themselves into the very heart of his Iowaland.

Captain Allen sent a report back to the army headquarters, "I have selected a point at the junction of the Des Moines and Raccoon rivers. The soil is rich and wood, stone, water, and grass are at hand. It will be high enough up the river to protect the peaceable Indians from the Sioux and in the heart of their best country. It is about equidistant from the Missouri and Mississippi. I propose to name the fort, Fort Racoon."

The army officials were shocked. Such a name as

Fort Raccoon would certainly be in bad taste. They suggested that it be named Fort Des Moines, even though there was already a fort by that name in Iowa.

Captain Allen explained to the Indians what he proposed to do. They listened; then Chief Pash-e-pa-ho replied in a sad farewell to his hunting grounds, pledging that the Sac and Fox would be friendly, "I say welcome. Good bye." He led his warriors westward from the Raccoon Forks to look for other hunting grounds. As the Indians left, the Dragoons stripped down a white birch tree for a flag pole, and soon the American flag was flying over the site of the new Fort Des Moines.

The fort was soon constructed of logs from the river banks. By fall the fort was completed. The Indians had agreed that they would all leave Iowa by 1845. On October 11, 1845, a cannon was fired at the new Des Moines Post and relayed across the sparsely settled land as a signal that the land was now in the possession of the white man. With this cannon shot Iowa's present city of Des Moines was born. Settlers soon poured into the area around the fort, and within a year or two there were so many settlers that the Dragoons' protection was no longer needed. Fort Des Moines was abandoned.

Other Iowa Forts

The Dragoons established other forts in Iowa. Fort Atkinson in Winneshiek County in northeastern Iowa was a unique fort in American history. It was built to protect Indians from Indians—the peaceful Winnebagoes from the warlike Sioux. This fort, constructed of limestone instead of the usual log fortifications, still stands on its high plateau above the little town of Ft. Atkinson and has recently been restored and preserved as a state park. Here can be seen the ammunition shelter, cannon house,

Fort Atkinson—a unique fort in history

and the officers' barracks. Fort Atkinson is one of the few early American fortifications still standing.

As the white settlers pushed westward, Fort Clark, later renamed Fort Dodge, was built on the Des Moines River below the mouth of Lizard Fork. Fort Croghan was built at Council Bluffs on the Missouri River. Following the Spirit Lake Massacre, during the Sioux outbreaks which followed in Minnesota, blockhouses and stockades were built at Correctionville, Cherokee, Peterson, Estherville, and Spirit Lake. As the white population increased and the Indians disappeared, the forts were soon abandoned. With the forts gone, the duties of the Dragoons were assumed by the sheriffs of the newly organized towns and counties of the state.

Lewis and Clark and Zebulon Pike explored the

boundaries of Iowa, but it was Kearney and Allen and the Dragoons who gave to the world the first account of internal Iowa. No doubt one of the most important results and aims of the military marches of the Dragoons was to impress the Indians with the power of the United State Government. Certainly the Indians were impressed, for word of the marches was passed from tribe to tribe whenever the Dragoons appeared.

The Dragoons opened up Iowa for the homesteaders. Assured of the protection by these brave watchmen, white settlers flooded into Iowa in the years that followed.

The Dragoons, mounted on their cavalry ponies, threading their way through the unsettled river valleys and across the bare prairie land, have long disappeared. Today, in their place, Iowa has 300 Highway Patrolmen led by their commanding officer keeping the peace across the state. These modern watchmen of the frontier promote and maintain highway safety, assist motorists in distress, and exercise police powers. Compared with the 1100 mile marches of the early Dragoons, the modern Patrolmen travel nearly ten million miles each year protecting the citizens of Iowa.

Chapter 14

THE SAINTS GO MARCHING ON

While the Dragoons were policing the territory and opening trails for settlement, a religious group called the Mormons pushed their way across southern Iowa from east to west. They, too, opened a trail for settlement.

Because the religious beliefs of the Mormons were very different, they had been persecuted wherever they settled. Although many Iowa settlers strongly disapproved of the Mormons, they were for the most part tolerated as they migrated across the state. If they had decided on permanent settlement here, the story might have been different.

Who were the Mormons?

It was in the dead of winter February 6, 1846, when the Mormons crossed the Mississippi River into Iowa. Feeling against the Mormons had been running high ever since the day their leader, Joseph Smith, had been shot and killed while he was in jail at Carthage, Illinois.

The Mormons had come to Illinois after they had been driven out of New York, Ohio, and Missouri. The official name of the group was "Church of Jesus Christ of Latter Day Saints" but they called themselves "Saints". Partly because of their religious belief that they alone were the chosen people of God, the Mormons had met with persecution wherever they tried to settle. In 1839 they came to a settlement in Illinois called Commerce, directly across the Mississippi from Montrose in Lee County, Iowa. They renamed the settlement Nauvoo, and by 1844 it had grown to a city of twenty thousand. Their prophet, Joseph Smith, proclaimed Nauvoo the seat of the church and began the construction of a million dollar temple.

Hostility toward the Mormons grew as the colony prospered. When the leaders announced that the Mormons would be permitted to have more than one wife, a storm of indignation arose among the non-Mormons around Nauvoo. It was whispered that the Mormons even harbored criminals. As the temple soared skyward, this visible evidence of their faith was matched by a growing resentment toward these people who said their faith was supreme. When Joseph Smith announced his intention of running for the President of the United States, the rest of Illinois began to fear the political strength of the city that in 1846 was bigger than Chicago.

Riots and violence broke out. Mobs formed. Joseph Smith and other Mormon leaders were arrested and jailed. Joseph Smith and his brother Hyrum were murdered by an angry mob while they were in jail at Carthage awaiting trial.

A New Leader

Who would be the leader now? Many tried to get the honor, but the choice fell upon Brigham Young. The task was not an easy one. The rioting had not stopped with the murder of Joseph Smith. Brigham Young knew that if they stayed in Nauvoo, the city would be sacked and burned. They must leave Nauvoo, of that he was sure. But where would they go? One thing Brigham Young knew for certain, it had to be far away from any settled part of the land.

After studying maps made by Lewis and Clark, he summoned the Saints to tell them they must prepare for a great migration.

"Our people have been driven out of their homes from New York to Illinois," he said. "Wherever we go, greed and hate and envy follow us. This time we will move so far away no one will be near us. We will choose a spot so desolate that no one will ever want it. We will go to a desert far out west beyond the mountains. We will get completely out of the United States!"

A murmur went through the crowd. Then the questions began to come. "A desert, Brother Brigham?" "Where will we get food?" "How will we get there?" The murmurs began to swell into disapproval.

"Silence!" roared Brigham. "Where is your faith? Of course the way will be long and it will be hard. We will have to cross fifteen hundred miles of wilderness and make our own trails, for there are no waterways. We will have to cross rivers that will have no bridges and we will have to cross deserts where there is no water at all. We will have to face danger, starvation, and disease. And some of us will die before we get there. But if we have faith, we will get to that desert. We will make it blossom. We will make it a haven for our people."

Brigham Young had spoken and the people listened. The thought of leaving their comfortable homes in Nauvoo and setting out across the unknown prairie to an unknown place beyond the mountains filled them with fear. But they did not doubt the wisdom of their leader, and they willingly followed his commands.

"Every family of five is to have one good wagon," Brigham told them, "three yoke of cattle, two cows, three sheep, one-thousand pounds of flour, twenty pounds of sugar, one rifle and ammunition, a tent and poles, from ten to twenty pounds of seeds, farming tools, cooking utensils and bedding."

Every home in Nauvoo began preparing for the long journey. Brigham Young kept urging them to work faster, for he was certain the time they had to prepare was short. Any day the mobs would come and force them to leave their city. The women knitted and sewed, the men made harness and built wagons. Brigham was everywhere. He went from home to home offering advice, cheering the faint-hearted, demanding top performance.

The Saints Move Out of Nauvoo

The river was beginning to freeze as Brigham ordered one thousand families across the Mississippi. As ice crunched along the sides, families with wagons and livestock were ferried across the river into Iowa. There they set up camp at Sugar Creek, nine miles from Nauvoo.

Each day marked the arrival of more Saints until many thousands had crossed the Mississippi to the Sugar Creek Camp. On February 16th, a blizzard suddenly descended from the northwest, and within a few hours the Mississippi was frozen solid. The remaining families drove their teams and wagons across the ice to safety. To the people who were fleeing from their enemies, this seemed very similar to the parting of the waters of the Red Sea.

To those at the Sugar Creek Camp, the twenty below zero weather brought much suffering. These people who were used to comfortably heated homes were now shivering in their canvas tents, wagon boxes, and brush huts. Snow fell so heavily that the paths between the tents and wagons had to be marked with sticks. Some families were destitute, had no covering at all, and had to sleep on the ground. Great log fires burned throughout the camp, but the wood was damp and smoked so badly it was impossible to get next to the fire.

Brigham Young went from one group to another, trying to give cheer here, making them double up there, dividing food supplies, carrying blankets to the sick. The coat that he could barely fasten only a few short weeks ago now overlapped twelve inches.

This was no place for anyone whose faith was weak. A few, beset by fears, broke away, but most of them, inspired by their leader, never doubted the wisdom of this tremendous venture. To everyone he spoke words of courage and this was enough. They were willing to follow him to the ends of the earth. The brass band had come across the river from Nauvoo. As the north wind howled around the camp and the snow piled in drifts around the huts and tents, Brigham ordered the band to play.

"Play a bright and a spritely tune," he said. With that the notes of a Scotch reel drifted through the camp. The people came out of their tents, miserable and half-frozen, but they began to sing. First the women sang, then the children and men, until the entire camp was filled with song.

Brigham Young stood listening with his friend, Heber Kimball. "We must not forget this," he said. "As long as our people can dance and sing, they will not be defeated."

Other uses were made of the brass band. They hired out to play concerts in the nearby settlements and received their pay in cash and foodstuff. Once the band split one hundred and thirty rails before they played a concert and traded them to the farmers for corn.

Other trading took place. As the Saints began to realize their wagons were overloaded, they exchanged possessions for food and livestock. One time Heber Kimball traded a feather bed for a cow.

The Westward Movement Begins

By March, snow still covered the ground, but winter showed signs of ending. Brigham gave the order to break camp and start moving west. Five hundred wagons followed the Des Moines River to Farmington. They halted for the night, scraped off the ground, and pitched their tents in the snow. They had begun the trail that was to be marked by graves as hundreds died and were buried along the wayside. Starting in Lee County, the Mormon Trail went through Van Buren, Davis, Appanoose, Monroe, Lucas, Decatur, Clark, Union, Adair, Cass and Pottawattamie counties to the Missouri River.

As often happens in Iowa, March was a month of severe weather changes. There were sudden thaws, turning the frozen earth into a sea of mud, followed by nightly freeze-ups. There were torrential rains followed by icy winds carrying snow and sleet. The trail was

The Mormon trails through southern Iowa

strewn with wagons broken or stalled in the bottomless mud and bones of animals that had fallen in their tracks.

A diary account records: "Some of our experiences during those days could not be written, neither could time erase them from my memory. . . the road lay over a prairie, and the earth became soft and inundated with a previous rain. All that could were obliged to walk to favor the poor animals. Our feet would sink in the mud at every step and some of us came near minus our shoes. As for umbrellas, they were rare articles, and we had the cold, pitiless rain beating down upon us all the way, till we were chilled and shaken with the cold. . ."

The travelers were not only drenched on the road but the mud was ankle deep around the tents. Floors of the tents were covered with brush to keep from sinking into the mud while they slept. Sometimes the weather would turn freezing cold during the night, and they would wake to find themselves frozen in the mud.

160

Dry clothing, warm bodies, and properly cooked food became luxuries to dream about.

One person wrote: "It has rained constantly for six days, and my bed clothing has never been dry during that time. Today I got my bedding out to dry for the first time."

Two months after leaving Nauvoo they came to some fertile land next to a beautiful place where they could set up camp. Grassy hillsides rolled away in all directions. It was so beautiful the Saints called it Garden Grove.

"We will stop here for awhile and rest," said Brigham Young. "Then we will build log cabins, plow this sod and plant this rich earth to corn, wheat, potatoes, and whatever else will grow."

Grateful for a rest, the Saints set up a permanent camp. While the planting and building were going on, others went in search of wild game. Some were splitting rails, building fences, and digging wells. Within a month Garden Grove was turned into a huge settlement that would be ready for the next group of Saints on the road behind them.

When the work was completed, they pushed on twenty-seven miles northwest to prepare another camp. Because they thought of it as a vision of the Promised Land, they called it Mount Pisgah. Again it was plow and plant until fifteen hundred acres were under cultivation. Cabins and a tabernacle were built, and again when they were finished, Brigham Young gave the call to move on west.

These Mormon camps put thousands of acres of Iowa prairie land under cultivation. Most camps, such as the one at Mount Pisgah, were the first white settlements in southern Iowa. Although the Mormons made temporary

Mt. Pisgah Cemetery at Lorimor

settlements, the cultivated land was quickly taken over by pioneers who came to stay.

While the Mormons were at Mount Pisgah, they were visited by Captain James Allen. Captain Allen had been sent out with the Dragoons in 1843 to locate a military post at the Raccoon Forks of the Des Moines River. Now, three years later, he was out recruiting soldiers. The United States was at war with Mexico and needed volunteers. When the Mormons realized the possibility of getting to their destination at government expense, the enlistments soon filled the quota of 500. The seven dollars a month army privates were paid was used by the Saints for food and equipment. Some Mormon women managed to enlist in the army as laundresses.

All that summer and fall different groups of Saints trudged wearily westward. For some, the rigors of the trail were too great. As a consequence of too little to eat, overwork, and exposure to the extreme weather changes, sickness and death became a common experience. Burials were made along the trail with the bark stripped from trees used for coffins. Besides those buried beside the trail, there were some 800 buried at Mount Pisgah.

Winter Quarters

Brigham Young had planned for winter quarters to be on the banks of the Missouri River, where Council Bluffs is now located. There he would get ready for the next leg of the journey the following spring. But he had not planned on all the Mormons leaving Nauvoo and following him. Instead of waiting for the crops to be harvested, they had set off across Iowa until there was an almost unbroken line clear across the state. By the time they had all reached the Missouri, there were some three thousand wagons and carts, thirty thousand head of cattle, hundreds of horses and mules, and at least sixteen thousand Saints. Together with the ones with Brigham, there were over twenty thousand people to make preparations for before winter set in.

With the Saints on both sides of the Missouri River, Brigham Young organized every camp until every man knew exactly what he was to do. Almost overnight the village of Kanesville sprung up on the Iowa side. This later became the city of Council Bluffs. Across the river they set up quarters at Florence, now a suburb of Omaha. The following spring they started their long trek to the valley of the Great Salt Lake. All through the

A Mormon Trail Memorial

next several years they continued to migrate through Iowa to the Promised Land.

The Handcart Expedition

But the strangest method of getting to Utah was still to come. The church had made many converts in Europe who wanted to come to America to join the Saints in Utah. Some thirteen hundred of these converts arrived in Iowa City the summer of 1856. The railroad ended there. Having no money to outfit themselves with horses and wagons, they found there was only one way to complete the journey—to walk.

They camped west of Coralville and began making handcarts. These carts were made with two wheels with the box the width of a wagon and three or four feet long.

164

A crossing on the Mormon Trail

There was a crossbar in front with which to push or pull the cart. It was all made out of Iowa hickory except an iron rim for the tires.

Pushing their handcarts, the first group left Iowa City in June of 1856 with four more groups leaving throughout the summer. Walking from early morning until late at night, they were able to average from twenty-five to thirty miles a day, which was twice the average of ox-teams. They presented an almost inhuman sight as the women and children were hitched to the carts as well as the men. Sometimes whole families worked at moving the cart with some pulling, some pushing, and the small children trudging along in the dust by the side. Only very small children and the sick were allowed to ride in the cart.

The first three groups had arrived in Salt Lake by October, but the last two groups ran into difficulty. Starting too late, they got caught in South Pass in a snowstorm. Short of provisions, they were already weak.

165

Death began to take its toll as they were exposed to the freezing weather. Sixty-seven people in the fourth group died and one-fourth of the people in the last company.

The arrival of these starving people in Salt Lake caused the handcart method to be abandoned. As the railroad tied the nation together, migration by handcart came to an end.

Not all the Mormons left Iowa when Brigham Young issued the call for all the Saints to come to Salt Lake. A group of them had formed their own colony under the leadership of Joseph Smith's son. They called themselves the Reorganized Church, and they settled at Lamoni in Decatur County. Graceland College, established in 1895, became a center of culture for their faith. With their high educational standards and their deep religious belief, they have added much to the cultural pattern of the state.

Although Iowans generally regarded the Mormons with suspicion, there was never an open outbreak of hostility against them. There may have been several reasons for this. For one thing, the Mormons were migrating rather than making permanent settlements. Another fact was that the trail crossed southern Iowa, a part of the state not yet settled.

The path of migration used by the Saints became known as the Mormon Trail. Highways follow the route across southern Iowa today. Because it was such a clearly marked trail, it was used by settlers coming into Iowa and helped promote the rapid settlement of that area.

Chapter 15

THE SEVEN VILLAGES
OF THE AMANAS

The unmistakable sound of building echoed across the Iowa River valley. As the steady stroke of the hammers mingling with the whining sound of saws going through hard wood filled the air, Christian Metz stood back and watched with satisfaction. This new village of Amana was rapidly taking shape.

"We aren't going to be without homes very long, Brother Metz." An elder had stopped beside Christian Metz to survey the building.

"And I'll grant you no one will be homesick for Ebenezer," Christian Metz stretched his hand out toward the village. "Take a look at that street, with the houses all facing each other. Look down at the end of the street where the farm buildings are being built. And look at this end where the factories will be. Two weeks after our people get here, they'll forget all about our villages in New York. This looks just like Ebenezer."

" 'Tis a good way to build a village," agreed the elder. "Looks just like a village in Germany too. A solid looking village it is. Looks as if it were built to last."

"We'll be happy here," promised Christian Metz. "We won't be pushed out of this valley. We're here to stay."

"We're here to stay!" Christian Metz let his thoughts dwell on those words as he went back to pick up his hammer. He knew that life in this fertile Iowa valley was going to be good.

Life hadn't always been good. Christian Metz thought about the anxious years when they had left Germany. He and his group had different religious beliefs from the official German church. Under his leadership they came to the United States. Calling themselves the "Community of True Inspiration", they established a settlement near Buffalo, New York, and named it Ebenezer. The people who made up this community were stern, sober-thinking individuals who believed that life could be lived best by staying away from the influences of the world.

Their way of thinking was reflected in their speech and dress. Speaking only German, they spent no time in idle talk. Words were something to be used only when you had something to say and were not to be wasted. Both men and women dressed in somber colors, usually black, with the women wearing long dresses covered by huge aprons with a shawl around the shoulders and a bonnet tied under the chin.

They thought of themselves as a community of people who were bound together by the same beliefs. It simplified their living if they could own everything in common. Some could furnish money, some could furnish only labor, but by thrifty handling of what they

168

had, they were able to set up woolen mills and other industries. It was not long before they prospered.

But the outside world was pushing in on them as Buffalo, New York, continued to expand. Christian Metz came to a decision.

"We must move from Ebenezer," he announced to the elders. "The world is moving in too close. If we are going to maintain our own way of life, we must be isolated from the modern world."

The elders nodded in agreement. They had already seen evil influences creeping in. They must get their young people away from here. But where would they go? Anxiously they listened to Christian Metz.

"We will go West," he declared. "We will send a committee out West. We can find land that is cheaper and perhaps land that is just as good as our farms here in New York."

And so it happened that after exploring the possibilities of many areas the choice fell upon 26,000 acres of land in the fertile valley of the Iowa River. At the time the purchase was made in 1855, the area was almost inaccessible. The evil influences of the outside world would not penetrate this haven! The railroad ended at Iowa City, the state capital.

Moving to Iowa

Moving their possessions from Iowa City to their new home twenty miles west was done by ox-cart. They moved everything they owned to this unbroken prairie land. Looms from the woolen mills, farm machinery, household furnishings, livestock—a whole community— was taken down in New York and reassembled in Iowa.

The elders stood and surveyed the scene. This was indeed God's country! Very few spots on earth had rich black soil such as this. It did not even need clearing . It

169

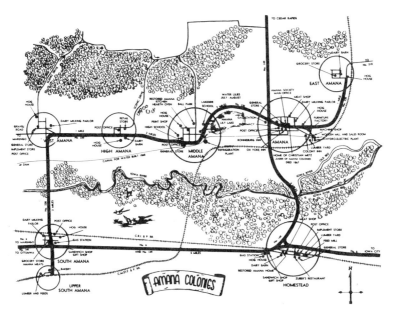

The Amana Colonies

stretched out endlessly, waiting for the turn of the plow. These German people knew good land when they saw it!

The Iowa River coursed through the bottom land with ledges of sandstone along the river and bluffs on either side of red and yellow clay. As far as the eye could see, timbers of hickory, of oak, and of walnut thickly clustered the hillsides. The clay for brick, the stone, the hard wood were all there, waiting to be used for building.

And finally the river itself was there to be used as a source of power to run their mills. It would not be long before the woolen mills taken down in Ebenezer would be busily humming once again.

Amana was the first village to be laid out in 1855. Christian Metz chose the name. It means to "believe faithfully". During the next seven years, five more vil-

An Amana farmstead

lages were built within a radius of six miles: West, South, High, East, and Middle Amana. In 1861 the railroad started pushing westward from Iowa City to a post office establishment called Homestead. The Amana elders purchased the village in 1865 and it became the seventh Amana.

An Amana Village

Each village was built on the same plan. At one end were the farm buildings with the factories at the other. In between was one long street with the general store,

An Amana house—simple and unadorned.

the meeting house, the kitchen house, and the homes. Houses, factories, stores, and meeting houses all looked the same. Only the size distinguished one from the other.

While the most commonly used building material was brick, made from the plentiful clay, frame houses were made also. But whatever the building material, the style was the same: simple, unadorned two-story buildings with twin gables and windows with small panes. If the buildings were frame, they were not painted. Wood did not need to be painted to be preserved, the elders said. It was cheaper to rebuild than to buy paint. Lumber and labor were free, but paint had to be purchased.

The Amana house was different from a regular house because there was no kitchen. All the food was prepared in the kitchen house, and the women took their turns working there. As many as fifty people could eat together in the large dining rooms. Families, if they wished, could carry baskets to the kitchen house to get food for a meal and eat it in their own homes.

Living in the Amanas was different from any other place. Each family was given a place to live according to its size. There was no rent to pay. Neither did anyone pay for their food and clothing. The doctor did not charge a fee for illness nor was there any funeral expense. The church was the government so there were no police and no courts. The church directed the farms and factories and saw to it that everyone worked. Fourteen years of age was considered the time to start doing the work of an adult.

Certain jobs became the work of certain families. The cabinet maker taught his son with pride and patience the ancient craft of making a beautiful piece of furniture out of the cherry and the walnut wood. And while agriculture and the woolen mills were the two main industries of the colonies, there were other smaller businesses to be maintained as well. The Amanas were self-sufficient and many kinds of jobs required doing. There were the shops where the ham and bacon must be smoked, the bakery where round crusty loaves of Amana bread must be baked fresh each morning, the harness to be made and mended, the wood to be cut for the saw-mills and the cleaning crew that had a never-ending job of white-washing. Each person took the job assigned to him and hoped he would be able to do his work well.

Children in the Amanas lived a simple, sheltered life. School was a place to learn to read German so the catechism could be learned and they could take part in the services of the church. Everyone went to school until they were fourteen. At that age they were given regular jobs in the Society. Boys would follow the craft of their fathers, and the girls would start taking their turn at the kitchen house. Occasionally an exception would be made. Doctors, dentists, teachers, and other professional people were needed by the Society and this required additional training. Gravely the elders made the choices of the ones who would be sent to the outside. The Society paid for their training and they knew their duty was to return to the Amanas and give their services as soon as they completed their training.

Religion was the substance that glued the Amana Society together. Working and going to church were the two activities of the villages. There was an average of eleven church services a week. The church was as plain as the people who attended it. Bare white-washed walls, unpainted benches scrubbed to a bleached white, the simple table in front covered with a green cloth gave an atmosphere of humble worship. Men and women entered by separate doors and sat on different sides of the church. The women wore little caps, a shoulder shawl and an apron, all in black. Elders who conducted the business affairs of the villages also conducted the church services. The Bible lesson, the hymns, the sermon, the prayers were in German.

For eighty years the Amana colonies prospered. They seemed to have solved the problems that plagued the rest of the world. Everyone was employed, their needs were well supplied, they had a high standard of living, they enjoyed contentment. There were no slums, no juvenile delinquents, no jails.

The Outside World Creeps In

But the world was creeping in on them nevertheless. Even by 1900 it was becoming apparent that this carefully chosen spot was not isolated from the world after all. The Community of True Inspiration may have moved by ox-cart in 1855, but six years later the railroad had gone through. Then a road scarred the prairie as it followed the capital from Iowa City to Des Moines. By 1910 the automobile was changing the face of America, and the River-to-River[1] road passed through the Amana colonies. In 1930 a long gray ribbon of concrete unfolded through Homestead, then split off like a forked tongue toward Cedar Rapids and Iowa City. The isolation of the Amanas was no more.

As the world came to them, the people of the colonies became less and less satisfied with their simple way of life and began demanding the luxuries from the outside. This, coupled with the depression of the 1930's, brought about the need for a change.

And so it was in June, 1932, the old Amana Society

[1] A highway going from the Mississippi to the Missouri River.

went out of existence and the new Amana came in. The church became a separate institution and the new Society became a giant business corporation. Members were given shares of stock in the company according to their years of service. They were then free to buy their homes and earn wages and spend their earnings on cars, radios, and new kitchens.

Amana Today

The appearance of today's Amana has changed somewhat since the sandstone and brick buildings were built a century ago. The charm of an old-fashioned German village is partly lost by the new houses being mixed in with the old. The modern buildings of the Amana Refrigeration Company make a sharp contrast to the dormitory-like Amana houses close by. But the riot of color from the old-fashioned flower beds is as gay as ever, and the grape vines climb their sturdy trellises to prove each year that even a vine must prove its worth by producing fruit as well as ornamental leaves.

Modern methods have been introduced into the factories, but many of the old values remain. To own a piece of furniture made in the Amanas is still to own a treasure. Amana woolens are a possession to be prized, and Amana freezers are known across the nation for their high quality.

The kitchen houses may be gone, but in their place has come the Amana restaurant. German food served family style is an unforgettable experience for anyone who has ever eaten there. "Eating at the Amanas" has become an Iowa pastime.

It is only in the church that Amana remains the society of the past. The sanctuary is still the plain, unadorned worship center of old. Men and women go in

A bit of Old World Germany still remains in Iowa

their separate entrances and sit on different sides of the church, the women wearing the black cap, shawl and apron. The elders sit behind the plain table and conduct the service in German. The number of services has dwindled to two a week where there were formerly eleven. This too may pass away.

The Amish of Iowa

Many times the Amana people are confused with another group of German settlers in Iowa called the Amish. The name is similar, the nationality the same; they fled to America because of persecution, but there the similarity ends. The Amanas resisted the intruding world until 1932, but the Amish, or "Hook and Eyes" as they are termed, are still resisting progress.

Coming to Iowa in 1839, these Mennonite groups are found in western Buchanan County and eastern

The "plain people" of Iowa—the Amish

Black Hawk County. It is a strange sight to see a horse pulling a buggy, clopping down the highway, and even stranger to see seated in the buggy a bearded man wearing a broad-brimmed hat and his wife in bonnet and shawl. The "plain people", they are called. These unadorned people stay away from all amusements, high school and college, and other people. Church services are held in the homes. Their farms are well kept, their large houses and farm buildings are painted and in good repair. All around is an air of prosperity. Not in keeping with this prosperous look is the absence of electricity, telephones, and motorized machinery. The simple life is their way of keeping close to the Word of God.

They do not believe in education beyond the eighth

177

grade. Not wanting an "outsider" teaching their young people, they have not been able to staff their schools with Amish teachers who have certification requirements. With educational standards becoming ever higher in the state and the one room school going out of existence, these God-fearing people are found breaking the Iowa school laws. Some of the Amish elders have gone to jail rather than submit to having their young people attend reorganized schools. To the Amish, this would be breaking a higher law: a religious law.

Some Amish families have considered moving out of the state, perhaps to Mexico, where they would be allowed to follow their beliefs without interference.

The people of the Amana Colonies and the Amish brought a bit of Old World Germany to the Iowa countryside. With their thrifty, industrious habits, they added to the wealth of the state. With their deep devotion to their faith, they added to Iowa's religious culture.

Chapter 16

FROM ANCIENT LANDS

As the frontier opened up for settlement, pioneers came pouring into Iowa from a restless Europe that was just emerging from the Napoleonic era. The immigrants representing every religious, political, and social belief made up the pioneer groups. They were attracted by the reports of the rich soil, the cheap land available for homesteading, and a chance to establish a new life for their family. People who still held to their old European traditions saw in Iowa a place to transplant a bit of their own native land without interference from government or neighbor.

Iowa was, in fact, the first area in the northern part of the Louisiana Territory that attracted settlers. An ad in an eastern newspaper had reported, "Taking in consideration the soil, the timber, the water, the climate, the Iowa Territory may be considered the best part of the Mississippi Valley."

The first large body of foreigners to enter Iowa was a group of over 800 Hollanders, who set out in four sailing

"But where IS Pella?" asked Mareah Scholte.

vessels the year after Iowa became a state. Led by Dominie[1] Henry P. Scholte, the 160 Dutch families landed in New York and crossed the eastern part of the United States by rail, canal boat, and river steamer until they arrived in Keokuk. From here they made their way by wagon, horse, and on foot, following the Mormon Trail, to an 18,000-acre plot of land in Marion County.

Nailed to a tall pole set out in the middle of the prairie was a sign: "Pella".

Mareah Scholte, the dominie's wife, looked at the sign and then around at the vast expanse of unsettled prairie.

[1] Dominie was a term meaning *master*.

"But where *is* Pella?" she asked.

"We are in the center of it, my dear," answered the dominie.

The Iowa prairie land with the tiny cabin squatting in the long grass was far different from the lovely home she had left in the Netherlands. Mareah was used to the gay social life of a finishing school in Paris where she had proven to be a talented musician and artist. Homesick and discouraged, she turned to unpack the trunk containing her Delft china, which she had packed so carefully to bring to the strange new land. She lifted the lid. In the bottom of the trunk lay her lovely dishes shattered to bits by the long journey from Holland.

After a few tears shed for the broken dishes, Mareah turned away and announced firmly, "I shall make a pathway of them from this old log cabin to our new house." And she did. The Scholtes had the only front walk in America made from genuine Delft china!

Like the Pilgrim Fathers, the Hollanders were Separatists, who were seeking religious freedom in the rolling prairie land on the divide of the Des Moines and Skunk rivers. In fact, some of the families who came to Pella were remnants of the Puritans of Holland. In the group were merchants, craftsmen, teachers, farmers, as well as artists and poets.

During the first years of Pella's existence, the town came to be known as "Straw Town", for the Hollanders were forced to improvise houses: dug-outs covered with straw or hay, and even homes built entirely of straw.

In Pella each man worked for himself. Each citizen was an individual. In some cases they did not even agree upon their religious beliefs. The industrious Hollanders soon built churches and schools, and within a

Tulip Festival Time at Pella

few years they had established one of Iowa's first colleges, now called Central College.

Many other friends in Holland decided to join the group in Marion County. So many came from Holland that the group decided to form another settlement. Henry Hospers took over the leadership of this group and settled in Sioux County in northwest Iowa. They named their settlement Orange City, in honor of William of Orange, a king of the Netherlands. These Hollanders also set up a college which is known today as Northwestern College.

Even today Pella and Orange City remain predominantly Dutch. Each spring these communities revive their old world ties by staging their famous tulip festivals.

182

Street-Scrubbing is a tradition of the Tulip Festival

Norwegians at Decorah

Sometime later a group of Norwegians chose to settle in Winneshiek County and founded the town of Decorah in northeast Iowa. Like the Dutch of Pella and Orange City, the citizens of Decorah held close to the customs of their native land. Songs, artwork, and hand work have kept alive the Norwegian heritage. Many children of this community still are taught to read, speak, and write the Norwegian language.

Just previous to the Civil War, Luther College was established in Decorah, and today it is one of Iowa's leading small colleges. A reminder of the close bond which has always existed between Decorah and its mother country is the Norwegian-American Historical Museum, which includes many exhibits of national interest. Norwegian royalty has honored this section of Iowa with their visits on various occasions.

The Irish In Iowa

A failure in the potato crop in Ireland, coupled with the hatred of English rule in Ireland, caused a migration of many Irish to Iowa. Many of the Irish settled in Emmetsburg, named for their national hero, Robert Emmet. In recent years the town has played host to the Mayor of Dublin, Ireland, at their annual St. Patrick Day's celebration. Another Irish settlement was made at Cascade in Delaware County.

Cedar Rapids And The Czechs

In the early 1850's a large number of Czechs began to settle on both sides of the Cedar River and helped to swell the population of the growing city of Cedar Rapids. The Czechs were particularly skilled as tailors, bakers, butchers, and farmers. As a group the Czechs were industrious and thrifty. Many Czechs in Cedar Rapids still speak their native language and adhere to the "old country" customs.

Many Czech activities and organizations are carried on in Cedar Rapids as well as farther north in the little town of Spillville. Spillville was Anton Dvorak's home during the period that the composer was writing his

184

famed "New World Symphony". Here too, a fine example of old world craftsmanship can be seen in the Bily Brothers exhibit of hand-carved clocks of all types and sizes.

The English At LeMars

In the latter part of 1876, a young Englishman came to the United States to take part in a rowing contest. Impressed by the large amount of land available for homesteaders, the young man, William B. Close, purchased 30,000 acres of land in Plymouth County. Soon other English noblemen joined the wealthy young Englishman until nearly 500,000 acres were laid out into large estates. The Englishmen built fine homes and attempted to establish the fine style of living that they had known on their estates in England with fox hunts, servants, race horses, and even cricket greens. But the severe winters of Iowa soon discouraged the young noblemen, and they divided their estates and sold them and returned to England. LeMars still bears traces of the proposed English society.

Other Racial Groups

Many other national groups settled together throughout the Iowa frontier: the Welsh at Williamsburg, the Scots at Ida Grove, the Swedish people in Henry and Boone County, Hungarians in Decatur County, the French in northeast Iowa, and the Germans in southeast Iowa. Most of the members of these groups came directly from Europe to Iowa after receiving encouraging letters from their friends and relatives in the new settlements.

The Gaps Between the Racial Settlements

These settlements by racial groups, however, were

spotted throughout the state, but filling in the large areas between were many pioneer farmers who had previously settled in states east of the Mississippi such as Pennsylvania, Ohio, Indiana. When news of richer soil and cheaper land reached these restless frontier followers, they packed their household goods in a covered wagon and started west again. They discovered that in Iowa they could grow corn and raise livestock. Many of these people were Germans and Scandanavian. They were good farmers, and as they settled down they helped to bring about stable conditions in the fast developing state.

John Deere had invented the steel plow in 1837, and Cyrus McCormick the reaper in 1831. The new machinery spurred greater production, and Iowa soon became dotted with homesteads from border to border.

A Part of the United States

During the years Iowa was becoming a territory and then a state, the United States almost doubled in size. The restless pioneers, believing a great part of the Louisiana Purchase not suitable for settlement, had looked to the far West and thought it their destiny to make all the land to the Pacific Ocean a part of the United States.

While Iowa, Wisconsin, Illinois and Minnesota were still thinly populated in 1840, the southern part of the Mississippi Valley had become settled. The climate and soil in that area were ideal for the raising of cotton.

Texas was a part of the area around the Gulf of Mexico where cotton grew well. Americans had been going into Texas since 1820. Texas rebelled against the Mexican government and became independent in 1836. In 1845 Texas was admitted to the Union as a slave state.

During this period pioneers had also been following the Oregon Trail and settling in the Oregon Country. It was claimed by both Britain and the United States. In 1846, the same year Iowa became a state, the United States and Britain agreed to divide the territory.

The Mexican War was fought 1846-1848 and the United States received New Mexico and California. By 1848, with but few minor changes, the United States had reached the size it is today.

Up to this point there had been a balance of free and slave states coming into the Union. This additional territory raised some questions. What about slavery in this new area?

Congressmen who were opposed to slavery tried to get a law passed forbidding the extension of slavery into the territories. They failed, but it did not settle the argument. In 1850 a Compromise was passed saying the new territory could vote to be slave or free. Another part of the Compromise set up a more efficient method of returning runaway slaves to their owners. This caused the Underground Railroad to grow throughout the northern states.

Emotions began to reach a high pitch as thousands of Northerners read *Uncle Tom's Cabin,* published in 1852. They became convinced that all slaves were treated as those who were characters in the book.

A bill called the Kansas-Nebraska Act was passed in Congress allowing Kansas and Nebraska to organize as separate territories and to vote to come in free or slave. This caused the organization of the Republican party whose members were pledged to keep slavery out of the territories.

Iowa was settled by people from both the North and the South, and there were people in Iowa who believed in slavery. There were a few slaves in Iowa although slavery was never legal. Iowa was a part of the territory declared free by the Missouri Compromise.

As the population of Iowa continued to grow after 1840, the number of Easterners and foreign immigrants outnumbered the Southerners. After 1854, Iowa was taken over politically by the Republican party and became anti-slavery. This, coupled with the presence of such groups as the Quakers in the state, made Iowa an active area of the Underground Railroad.

Chapter 17

LUCAS OF PLUM GROVE

"Why he looks like old Andy Jackson!" shouted Mayor George Beeler as he watched the *Brazil* ease into the Burlington wharf.

It was the year 1838.

Robert Lucas, newly appointed governor of the Territory of Iowa, stood on the deck of the steamboat and surveyed the crowd assembled to welcome him. He did resemble Andy Jackson with his white hair swept back from a high forehead and his stern, military bearing.

What a trip it had been! All the way from Cincinnati! Two months, it had taken. They had been stranded on sand bars in the Ohio River, low from the summer's drought. Then on the Mississippi there had been storms.

He sighed. He was 57 years old, and here he was starting out again on the very edge of civilization to organize a new government. He would have to admit, though, that he had done many things in those 57 years: soldier, surveyor, justice of peace, state representative,

state senator, governor, and now the governor of this new land.

He stepped off the boat and walked the length of the wharf. An important-looking young man came forward to greet him.

"Governor Lucas. I am William B. Conway, Esquire, the Secretary of the Iowa Territory."

Governor Lucas eyed him critically.

"Since you were so long in arriving," the young man continued, "I have taken it upon myself. . ."

That morning Governor Lucas discovered that Conway had "taken upon himself" all the duties of the Territorial Governor. Thus began the feeling of ill will between the Governor and his Secretary that was to mar the first years of Lucas' term of office.

Brusquely turning down the invitation to attend a banquet arranged for him by Secretary Conway and ignoring Conway's suggestions for further governmental procedure, Lucas announced pointedly that he would proceed at once to tour the new Iowa Territory with the purpose of deciding where the capital should be located.

True to his word, the next day Governor Lucas set out on a twelve day trip of the Territory. The Territory of Iowa was then three times the present size of Iowa. It included the present states of Iowa, North Dakota, South Dakota, and all of Minnesota west of the Mississippi River. Most of the population, however, was located along the west bank of the Mississippi River.

Going up river by steamer, the Governor stopped at all the little settlements. Crowds lined the shore to greet him. On the return trip, the Governor and his party traveled by farm wagon down to Davenport and Muscatine. Lucas had always been a farmer, and he felt quite at home jolting along behind a team of work horses.

At Agency he met the great chief, Keokuk, and listened with respect to the diplomat's oration. Returning to Burlington, he announced that he had reached a decision on the location of the capital. The capital would be Burlington, and the new Zion Methodist Church would serve as the temporary capitol building.

Only after this, did Governor Lucas accept the invitation to his welcoming banquet. Speaking before the men who would frame the first Iowa government, he

191

said, "It will be my great pleasure to cooperate in the framing of the laws and in laying the foundation upon which the future state of Iowa shall stand." The new Territory of Iowa was hardly formed when its citizens began to talk of statehood.

From the first encounter on the Burlington wharf, Governor Lucas was at odds with his Secretary over matters ranging from territorial elections to the purchase of pen knives and tin cups for the legislators. At times the stern, old governor was at odds with his own Iowa citizenry. Lucas was an old man in a young man's land. He was well experienced in matters of government, but he often assumed a domineering manner which was not appreciated by the young independent frontiersmen.

The Honey War

Governor Lucas' second year was one of more trouble —border trouble. Two different surveys had been made of the southern boundary between the Territory of Iowa and the State of Missouri, but the lines did not agree. The land in dispute was a strip of land thirteen miles wide across the southern boundary. The people in this area considered the land as part of the Iowa Territory. One part of the dispute concerned several trees along the Des Moines River that had honey stored in their hollow trunks. Honey was prized as a sweetening on the frontier, where sugar was expensive and scarce. A Missourian crossed the border and chopped down three of the trees and ran off with the honey. This act enraged the Iowans. They sent the Iowa sheriff after the man . . . and the stolen honey.

About the same time Missouri ordered its officers to collect taxes in the area claimed by Iowa. The Van Buren County settlers refused to pay and arrested the

Missouri sheriff sent over to assist the collectors. Missouri sent out its state militia to rescue the sheriff.

Governor Lucas was experienced in handling this type of dispute. He had settled just such an argument when he was governor of Ohio. The Territory of Iowa had no organized militia, but at Lucas' call for volunteers, 1200 frontiersmen equipped with pitchforks, log chains, squirrel rifles, and shotguns trooped toward Farmington. Only 500 reached the front, for by that time Governor Lucas and the governor of Missouri had agreed to submit the dispute to the United States Congress.

The armies soon disbanded and the Honey War ended without the firing of a single shot. The boundaries were finally established by a Supreme Court decision in 1851, and Iowa kept its honey trees.

Iowa City Becomes the Capital

With settlers pouring into Iowa, the citizens felt that the time had come to establish a permanent capital. The legislators decided that the capital should be located somewhere in Johnson County along the Iowa River. A committee of three members was appointed to select a site in that area.

A meeting of the commission was called for May 1, 1839, in the town of Napoleon, a tiny settlement of only a few scattered cabins. On the appointed day, only one commissioner appeared—Chauncey Swan. The loyal Johnson County settlers waited expectantly throughout the morning, but still the other two members of the commission did not arrive. By noon the crowd began to get restless. What if the other two commissioners did not come that day? Would the government take the capital away from Johnson County and give it to some other county?

The frontiersmen decided something must be done. Why not go after the two commissioners? But John Ralston lived too far away—over in Des Moines County. Wouldn't two commissioners make a majority? Why not go after John Ronalds, who lived just down the Iowa River? Philip Clark stepped out of the crowd. He would ride the thirty-five miles along the river and bring back Mr. Ronalds.

Through the afternoon into the early evening the crowd waited. Men drew watches from vest pockets and calculated the time it would take young Clark to make the ride. If he could just get back before midnight, everything would be legal.

The hours went by. Ten o'clock and no Clark. Eleven o'clock! Still Clark had not arrived. There were few settlements along the Iowa River, and wandering tribes of the Sac and Fox prowled the area. Clark may have been waylaid, or his horse may have become exhausted.

Reports vary on the exact hour that Clark and Ronalds galloped up from the river bank. Some say it was exactly one minute before midnight. Others say that if this were true, the night of May 1st was the longest and the early morning hours of May 2nd were the shortest they had ever experienced.

In any case, the two members of the commission met, called the roll, and adjourned until 10 o'clock the next morning. The capital of the Iowa Territory was saved for Johnson County.

After looking over the land, the two-member committee decided on a lovely hill overlooking the Iowa River. They marked it with a slab of wood, lettered:

Seat of Government
May 4, 1839
City of Iowa

The Old Stone Capitol at Iowa City

In the trees along the Iowa River the Mesquakie Indians watched, puzzled at the ceremony.

Work on the new capitol building began at once. Stone quarried from the hills along the Iowa and Cedar Rivers provided the material. The 4-ton blocks were floated downstream on log rafts, while guards kept a constant watch for lurking Indians. Robert Lucas was the orator that day, July 4, 1840, when the cornerstone was laid. The Stars and Stripes waved from atop the highest branch of an oak tree as he spoke of his faith in the future of the Iowa Territory.

The capitol building began to assume its shape in the

Plum Grove at Iowa City, home of Iowa's first Territorial Governor

pattern of the old Greek classic architecture. Timber of white oak, cut from the banks of the Iowa River, provided the framework. Inside a delicately carved circular staircase curved up the three-storied interior. On April 30, 1841, Governor Lucas ordered the capital officially moved from Burlington to Iowa City.

The move caused some confusion at first, for legislators had trouble finding the new capital city in the middle of the unsettled frontier. This was solved when Lyman Dillon was hired to plow a furrow from Dubuque to Iowa City to mark the route. Using a huge breaking plow and five yoke of oxen, Dillon plowed the 100-mile furrow. Perhaps it was symbolic that Iowa's first capital should be linked to the outside world by a new-turned furrow.

196

A town quickly sprung up around the new stone capitol building. One settler bragged that he was living in a cabin made of logs that only five days before had been growing in the woods. Not all houses built in the new capital city were log cabins, however.

Robert Lucas and his wife, Friendly Ashley Lucas, built a seven-room red brick house beside a plum thicket on the southeast edge of the town. The home, famous for having a fireplace in every room, was called Plum Grove.

Here at Plum Grove, Governor Lucas retired after serving out his three years as the first territorial governor. The Old Stone Capitol still stands on the banks of the Iowa River. Not far away is Plum Grove, preserved and restored as a monument to the man who laid the foundations for Iowa's government and prepared the way for statehood.

In 1966, the State Office Building on the Des Moines Capitol Grounds was officially named the Robert Lucas Building in honor of Iowa's First Territorial Governor.

Chapter 18

STAGECOACH DRIVER
—ANSEL BRIGGS

The driver lashed at the horses. The Concord coach rocked and jerked forward along the dusty road.

"Andrew ahead," shouted the driver. The horses had been walking at a leisurely pace most of the afternoon, but now that the stage was nearing the little Iowa settlement, the driver thought it necessary to enter at full gallop with the side horn sounding.

"Made her in record time!" shouted Ansel Briggs, as he swung down from the driver's box and handed the reins to the waiting stable boy.

A crowd of people had gathered, as usual, in front of the Butterworth Tavern. Although the little village of Andrew always waited with eagerness the arrival of the coach from Burlington, today the town was bursting with news of its own.

"Say Ansel," called Ansel's partner, John Francis, as

One of the few remaining stagecoach stops in Iowa

he dragged the leather mail bags down from the coach. "Some folks want to see ya over at the Tavern."

"Be right over," the driver answered. Then turning to the stable boy, he continued, "Have the boys down at the stable clean up this Concord. And have the jerky ready to roll first thing in the morning."

Ansel Briggs had done well since coming to Iowa from Vermont in 1836. In ten short years he had established a successful stage and mail route over the old Military Road between Dubuque and Burlington. He now owned two jerkies and a new Concord coach. The five-passenger jerky was a two-horse rig that could make the run to Dubuque and back once a week. . .and at a reasonable rate, Ansel figured: $3 per passenger, with baggage extra. Of course when it came to the Concord, Ansel himself drove the big nine-passenger deluxe stage, complete with driver's platform in front and a boot for luggage in the back. Ansel was proud of the Concord. Not many stagelines in Iowa could afford one like it.

Ansel strode over to the steps of the Butterworth

Tavern. A cheer rose from the crowd. Ansel looked bewildered.

"What's goin' on here?" he laughed.

John Francis raised his hands to get the crowd's attention.

"Ladies and gentlemen of Andrew. News has just come in by rider from Iowa City that Ansel Briggs of Andrew has been elected the first governor of the new state of Iowa."

The stagecoach driver looked amazed. He, the governor of Iowa?

"Speech! Speech!" cried the crowd.

Ansel Briggs looked out over the people gathered there. They were all his friends, he knew, but he was not much of a speechmaker. He had had little schooling, and he was not one for fancy words. He wasn't too sure how he felt about this governor's job. He was county sheriff of Jackson County now. . .but governor?

The whole thing had started with the remark he had made about banks. Everyone knew how worthless the paper money was that the Miner's Bank at Dubuque issued. Ansel always came back from that trip with a pocket full of it. What else but those wildcat bank notes from the Dubuque Bank was causing the hard times? Ansel had just plain told them down at Burlington, "No banks but the earth, and that well tilled."

"Speech! Speech!" the people kept clamoring.

Ansel moved to the top step of the Butterworth Tavern. He fixed his eye on the top of the little elm tree that he had planted himself in the middle of Andrew's Main Street, and began: "My friends. Having been called by my fellow-citizens to the office of governor of the State of Iowa, I enter upon its duties hoping that you will kindly extend to me your aid and indulgence."

200

As governor of the new state, Ansel Briggs knew that he would have to give up his mail and stagecoach contracts with the government. He felt, however, that it would only be a matter of a few years until the railroads would find their way into Iowa and the covered wagons and stagecoaches would fade into the distance. His stagecoaching days had been exciting, though.

The long trips from Dubuque to Davenport and to Iowa City, following the old Indian trials, were rough, but there were always the sights along the way: the moving prairie grass, the lone cabin, the lovely valley broken by a quiet stream. There were hazards too—prairie fires, Indians, breakdowns, accidents, and the Iowa mud up to the wheel hubs. Nothing could ever match the excitment of reining the horses at the stagecoach stop and throwing off the leather mail pouches.

If it were a noon stop, there would be two teams of four horses each, standing hitched and waiting to replace the tired team. If it were an overnight stop, on the other hand, nothing could be more welcome to the tired driver and his coachful of passengers than the smell of hot food and the prospect of a comfortable, clean bed awaiting them. Yes, he would hate to give it all up.

As the threats of Civil War hovered in the distance, every possible new state was watched closely with an eye to maintaining the balance of power between the slave and free states of the North and South. When Ansel Briggs appeared at the Stone Capitol in Iowa City to take the oath of office, he became the governor of the first free state to be admitted into the Union from the Louisiana Purchase Territory. To keep the balance, Florida was admitted slave along with Iowa in 1846.

The new governor decided not to move to the capital city. His wife had been ill, and the dampness of the Iowa

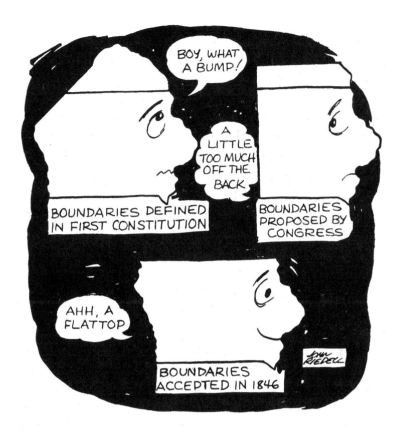

River town would not be healthful for her. This would mean that Ansel would have to ride horseback from Andrew to Iowa City to attend to the governmental business, but this he gladly did: more than 80 miles! His salary as governor of Iowa was $800 a year.

As Ansel glanced at the map of the new state over which he was to govern, he felt proud. "It's a well-shaped state. Her boundaries are good," he mused.

Not that they hadn't had trouble deciding on the final boundaries. There had been Governor Lucas' suggestions that Iowa extend as far north as to include the present cities of St. Paul and Minneapolis. The United States Congress thought Iowa would be too large with

202

these boundaries. They suggested the Nicollet boundaries that would have made Iowa extend two counties north into Minnesota and no farther west than the approximate location of Des Moines.

Finally the people of Iowa decided on the present boundaries. Ansel traced the boundaries on his huge wall map: from the Mississippi River west to the Missouri and Big Sioux Rivers, and north as far as the 43 degree 30" parallel. A good looking state, he concluded.

During Governor Briggs' term of office, Iowa saw a rapid increase in population. The Governor urged the establishing of common schools for everyone and suggested founding state-supported colleges for the training of teachers and farmers. He envisioned a great system of railroads, criss-crossing Iowa, and being well informed as an ex-stage driver and mail carrier, he recommended donating Iowa land to the railroad companies for this purpose.

With Iowa a state that now stretched from the Mississippi River to the Missouri, the question of relocating the capital once again came up for consideration. The frontier line had moved 80 to 90 miles westward. Iowa City was no longer a central point. Citizens of Iowa City were upset when Des Moines was chosen as the new capital. When the legislators established the State University at Iowa City with the Old Stone Capitol serving as the campus center, the citizens were satisfied. . . and well they should have been, for today Iowa City is fast becoming the center of culture for the Middle West.

One cold day a trail of wagons and bobsleds drawn by ten yoke of oxen started out from Iowa City across the bare prairie to Des Moines. Iowa government was moving again. In the sleds and wagons, piled high were the records, chairs, tables, desks, and even the safe

Stagecoach driver—Ansel Briggs

of the treasury of Iowa. The bobsled with the treasury's safe became stuck in a snow bank. It was necessary to abandon it for several days, but the safe finally arrived in Des Moines amid much rejoicing.

After serving as governor for four years that brought peace, prosperity, and growth to Iowa, Ansel Briggs mounted his horse for the last ride home to Andrew. His good friend, Senator Philip Bradley, accompanied him as he rode across the open prairie. The rhythmic clop-clop of the horses' hoofs wove itself into the sound of imagined voices from the past four years: "People may have questioned Ansel's spelling, but they could never

204

question his honesty." "You could always depend upon Ansel to pour oil on the troubled waters." "But I lack the essential knowledge drawn from public experience," "Please extend to me your aid and indulgence."

"Andrew ahead," called Bradley.

Ansel prodded his horse and the two galloped into the little main street with its young elm tree standing tall and firm in the center.

Chapter 19

JOHN BROWN AND THE
UNDERGROUND RAILROAD

"Young man! Do you know you are on free soil?"

The young slave turned and looked questioningly at the white man leaning over him. "Free soil?" he whispered.

"Yes, son. You're in Iowa. Tabor. Twelve miles north of the Missouri line. It's free soil."

"Free?" The slave stared at the man.

"You want to be free, don't you?"

The young Negro shook his head in disbelief. Of course he wanted to be free. Who wouldn't? But being free was something you dreamed about.

It was July 4, 1854. The young slave, along with five other slaves, had arrived in Tabor that afternoon with their master, Mr. Dennis, who was on his way from Mississippi to Salt Lake City.

"If you really want to escape, some of us fellows are going to see that you get a chance. You just wait.

Before night is over, we'll come after you." With these words, the strange man left.

The slave picked up the pails of water for his master and made his way slowly back to camp. He tried to crowd the words of the stranger out of his mind. This sort of thing didn't really happen, he was sure of that. But it *was* happening.

Even as the slave was carrying the water back to the wagon, a rescue party was being organized in Jesse West's blacksmith shop.

The night passed slowly. Mr. Dennis and his family were soon sound asleep. It was nearly one o'clock in the morning when five men slipped noiselessly into the camp. They motioned to the slaves.

Quietly the slaves followed the men out into the night to a point east of Tabor. In the blackness, with scarcely a sound, the group threaded their way across

A stop on the Underground Railroad

A cellar at Tabor once used on the Underground Railroad

the Nishna River on a huge cottonwood tree. On the opposite side of the Nishna, two men were waiting. Together the little group made their way, more rapidly now, northeast into Cass County. On the morning of July 6th they breakfasted at "Injun Town" with a Methodist missionary. The slaves were on their way to freedom.

This was the beginning of many incidents in Iowa that was to wear a path through the state. This path became a part of the Underground Railway with Tabor as the first station for the fugitives from Missouri.

John Brown Comes to Iowa

By the time John Brown came into the state in 1856, the Underground was well established. Many Quakers, who believed and practiced kindness toward others, lived in Iowa. The Quaker settlements became the way-stations on the way to freedom.

This was a ready-made situation for John Brown, for he had a dream. John Brown believed that it was his mission to free the slaves, and he had found the right people to help him—the Quakers.

On an October day in 1856, John Brown approached the little Quaker town of West Branch. He was weary, and the mule he was riding and the horse he was leading were also weary. Somewhere there must be a place to stop and rest. Ahead Brown saw a tavern: "Traveler's Rest." He climbed stiffly down from his mule and made his way to the door. He raised his hand to knock, but the door swung open.

"Welcome, friend," said a kindly-faced man. "My name is James Townsend. You look as if you could use something to eat and a good bed."

"Have you heard of John Brown of Kansas?" asked the visitor.

Everyone in the Quaker village had heard of John Brown. The landlord studied the tired man before him; then he took a piece of chalk from his vest pocket. Calmly he marked an "X" on Brown's hat, on his coat, and on his horse and mule. Brown understood the signal. He could stay at the tavern without charge.

"Sit down, sir," Mr. Townsend said, as John Brown

entered. "I'll soon have food for you that will make you forget your travels."

"Buckwheat cakes and sorghum!" John Brown's eyes glowed as he saw the stack of cakes placed before him. "It's been many a day since I've seen food such as this."

Cautiously the two men began to talk.

"We have heard rumors here in eastern Iowa," began Mr. Townsend, "that guns and ammunition have been sent to Tabor. Is this true?"

"It is true," replied Brown. "The rifles are stored in the basement of the home of the Congregational minister, the Reverend John Todd. I am going to find some way to make Kansas a free state. I am determined to bring about the overthrow of slave power."

"We Quakers do not believe in violence," warned Mr. Townsend gently, "but whatever we can do to give the poor black people their freedom, we will do gladly."

The next morning John Brown left West Branch. Eastern Iowa did not see John Brown again for more than a year, until late December in 1857. By this time he had changed his plan to strike a blow in Kansas and had decided to make an invasion somewhere in the East instead. He left Tabor with thirteen men in wagons drawn by mules. By the time he had reached the Quaker settlements of Springdale and West Branch, he had run out of money.

A farmer, William Maxson, took the little band in and provided work for the men on the neighboring farms. When they were not working in the fields, they drilled as an army. By spring, they were quick and strong. Young Quakers became a part of the group.

A real affection had sprung up between the Brown group and the Quakers. Before leaving for the East they all wrote their names on the white wall of the Maxson parlor. Many people thought they would never see John Brown in Springdale again, but they were mistaken.

John Brown's Raid Into Missouri

In the winter of 1858, John Brown returned to Tabor. A slave by the name of Old Jim slipped over the Missouri line. John Brown recognized him when he saw him coming into his camp.

"Old Jim, you are risking your life by coming here," John Brown greeted him.

"You've got to help us, Mr. Brown."

John Brown led him closer to the fire. "Tell me what is happening."

"They are going to sell us all. At auction. We're to be sold separately." Jim began to sob as he talked about being separated from his wife and children. "You must help us, Mr. Brown."

A daring plan was forming in John Brown's mind. They would raid across the Missouri border that very night and free the slaves that were to be auctioned off.

Scarcely taking time for any organized plans, the Brown party dashed into Missouri, took twelve slaves, horses, wagons, cattle and other property and hustled them into Nebraska. One slave owner was shot and killed in the skirmish.

By February 1859, the fugitive group had worked its way back into Iowa and reached Tabor. This time the citizens of Tabor were not wholly in sympathy with John Brown. They were as much against slavery as before, but slaves had been taken from their owners by force and there had been a killing. There was also stolen property. No, Tabor did not approve of such action. On the 11th day of February, the stolen slaves were sent

211

on their way long the line of the Underground Railroad. On the 18th, they went through Des Moines.

On the 20th of February, the forlorn little group straggled into Grinnell. John Brown went to find Mr. Josiah B. Grinnell, the founder of the town.

"My good friend!" Mr. Grinnell greeted John Brown warmly.

"I think your good friend is in a bit of trouble," answered John Brown.

"You mean what happened in Missouri?" asked Mr. Grinnell.

News as well as slaves traveled the Underground Railway.

Mr. Brown was given the best bedroom in Mr. Grinnell's house. The slaves were hidden in a barn nearby. The next day Brown was invited to speak in the Congregational Church.

But officers of the law were on the trail of John Brown. Rewards were being offered for his arrest. A plan had to be made to move the slaves out of town. With the help of Mr. Grinnell and some railroad officials, a freight car was left at West Liberty. Hurriedly the slaves and John Brown were taken to West Liberty and put into the freight car. When a passenger train arrived from the west, the freight car was attached. As the train eased out of the West Liberty station, John Brown was leaving Iowa for the last time.

When the train reached Davenport, the United States Marshall walked through the passenger cars looking for the stolen slaves. No one paid any attention to the freight car. The slaves were taken off the train at Chicago and were taken safely to Canada and freedom.

Later that same year John Brown attempted to seize the United States Arsenal at Harpers Ferry, Virginia.

His attempt failed, and he was hanged in December of 1859.

There are many places in Iowa where memories of John Brown can be brought alive. In the city park in Tabor, a bronze marker shows the place where John Brown and his men had a campground. The John Brown home still stands there. The Reverend John Todd home that was once used as a station for the Underground Railroad can still be seen in Tabor. The slaves were hidden in a small room under the eaves, and under the house is a long tunnel connected to the cellar.

The William Maxson farmhouse near Springdale, where John Brown and his men drilled as an army during the winter of 1859, remained standing for many years. Some of the belongings that were left in the Maxson farmhouse were divided among the members of the Maxson family. The eldest Maxson son received John Brown's sword, which is now the property of the Masonic Lodge in West Liberty.

All of the people of Iowa may not have agreed with John Brown's methods, but few would have quarreled with his motives. Many of the pioneer groups who settled the state were religious groups. The Quakers were only one of many religious faiths who believed that God had created man to be free. The Underground Railroad was the kind of help that could be provided.

George Washington Carver

Besides helping the slaves along the Underground Railroad, the people of Iowa gave another young Negro boy a chance. His name was George Washington Carver. He was born of slave parents in Missouri during the last year of the Civil War.

One night raiders galloped into the Missouri farmyard and kidnapped the Negro slave mother and her two-month old baby. The mother disappeared. Moses Carver, the owner of the stolen slaves, ransomed the tiny Negro baby by trading a $300 race horse for his return.

After the Civil War, all slaves were free, but George stayed on with Moses Carver. George was tiny and not able to do the heavy work in the fields, but he could make vegetables grow in the garden better than any one else. At the age of ten, George set out on his own to support himself, and above all, to get an education. The tiny Negro boy worked at jobs in Missouri and Kansas and attended school.

Upon graduating from high school, he was told that he could attend college in Kansas, but when he arrived he was not allowed to enter because he was a Negro.

George Washington Carver turned toward Iowa. Simpson College at Indianola accepted the frail Negro. George bought a washtub and found a woodshed. Here he washed and ironed shirts for the college boys so that he could raise money to attend college. His college professors were amazed at the boy's ability. The pictures that he painted in art class were so artistic that his teachers encouraged him to go to Paris and study art.

But George Washington Carver's fame was to come from a field far different. He could never forget how he loved to work in Moses Carver's garden when he was a tiny boy. He was fascinated by growing things, and much as he loved painting, he knew that plants and flowers must provide his field of research.

After three years at Simpson College, he enrolled at Iowa State College at Ames. When he graduated with a degree in agriculture, he was made a member of the college faculty and put in charge of the greenhouses. To teach at Iowa State College was a great honor for any man, black or white.

As much as George felt a great gratitude to the Iowa people, he could not forget his own people in the South. He felt he must return to help them, and he did. He taught the southern farmer how to raise peanuts and sweet potatoes in the fields worn out from cotton production. When the markets became flooded with peanuts, Carver looked around for new uses for the plant.

"Mister Creator," he said reverently, "what's a peanut and why did You make it?"

In seeking the answer to this question, George Washington Carver found 300 differents uses for the peanut. As his discoveries became famous, he was offered huge sums of money from various industries asking him to work for them. He never accepted any payment for his many discoveries. He gave them all to the world as a gift. He stayed in the South with his people all his life, but all of America benefited because Iowa gave this Negro boy a chance to get an education and to develop his talents.

Simpson College dedicated a new science building in 1956 to the memory of Dr. Carver: the first building in America on a predominantly white college campus to be dedicated to a Negro. At that dedication, Dr. Ralph Bunche, then Under-secretary of the United Nations, and a Negro said, "Carver, the Negro slave-born student, turned away elsewhere, found haven here in Simpson College, and for the first time came to know what it means to be accepted as a human being. It is impossible to calculate the good that has resulted from the social 'chain reaction' which began when Simpson College admitted this unimposing black man."

Chapter 20

CROCKER AND THE
IOWA BRIGADE

"Rebels Fire on Fort Sumter!"

The headline blazed across the *Burlington Hawkeye* that morning in May of 1861. The pony express, carrying the bundle of newspapers, galloped up the shores of the Des Moines River from Eddyville. Within eight hours the news had reached the capital city of Iowa.

Men soon gathered in serious groups on the streets wondering what was to become of the nation, now threatened by civil war. Someone called a massed meeting to be held in Ingham Hall.

That night the hall was packed with excited citizens. What should Iowa do and how could Des Moines help? Some thought that since the town lacked railroad connections, they should wait for further developments. A frail, young lawyer, sitting in the audience, listened to the arguments with growing restlessness. In a burst of enthusiasm, he leaped upon his chair and shouted, "We

216

have not called this meeting for speech making. We are now here for business. The American flag has been insulted, has been fired upon by our own people, but, by the Eternal, it must be maintained!"

There was a thunder of applause, but the young lawyer was not through. "I want now—just now—to raise a company to join the First Regiment of Iowa. I want a hundred men to come right up here and give their names to 'Hub' Hoxie, pledging themselves to go with me to Dixie!"

Within a few minutes, over a hundred young men had trooped to the front of the hall and volunteered to make up an Iowa brigade. This was the beginning of what was to become one of the crack regiments of the Civil War—the famous Crocker Brigade of Iowa.

Never Say Fail

Marcellus Monroe Crocker was ten years old when he migrated with his parents from Indiana to Illinois. Four years later the family moved to a little farm near the tiny village of Lancaster in Keokuk County. At the age of 16, Marc Crocker received an appointment to West Point, an honor for a boy so young.

The boy was never to complete his training at the United States Academy. He was called home by the death of his father. Marc, the oldest of the children, knew that he could never return to the life of a military cadet. His mother was alone on the Iowa farm with several younger children to support. In the severe winter of 1848-49, the boy chopped timber from the river banks, dragged the logs to the tiny log cabin, and chopped them in lengths for the fireplace.

The next year Marcellus moved his family into the village and supported them all by teaching school. At night he studied law by the light of a tallow candle. When news of Fort Sumter reached Des Moines, Marcellus M. Crocker had become a prominent young criminal lawyer. He had never known the meaning of the word "fail".

The hundred men who volunteered that night in Ingham Hall elected Crocker to be their captain. In a short time their enthusiastic leader had his company well drilled in the ways of army life. The regiment left Des Moines to be mustered in at Keokuk. The entire community assembled near the old Methodist Church in Keokuk to see the young volunteers off.

The 13th Iowa, the Crocker regiment, was sent down the Mississippi to St. Louis. The winter was spent at Jefferson City, guarding the state from Rebels, freezing in their tents, and sick in hospitals. For Crocker it was a time of preparation. Crocker routed out his men in the early morning hours and spent the day drilling and instructing them in field maneuvers. Late at night the eager captain discussed field tactics with his officers.

In a letter which Crocker wrote to Governor Kirkwood of Iowa during this winter in Jefferson City, he reported, "The regiment is now in fine condition; the boys have about recovered from the measles and mumps, and consider themselves ready for service. We do not wish the people of Iowa to understand or believe that we are at all uncomfortable or unhappy. Certainly we are not. If they will visit our camp of an evening they will find as jolly a crowd as they ever visited and will be astonished at the immense amount of music and fun."

In March they joined the army of General Grant and by the 6th of April were in the middle of the battle of Shiloh. The first day they saw ten hours of uninter-

218

rupted fighting, but the dauntless Captain Crocker re-grouped them for the next day's assault.

In the battle of Shiloh, there were more men from Iowa in proportion to the population of the state than any other state in the North. Eleven full regiments of Iowa volunteers made up the major part of the battle. There had not been a braver nor a cooler man on the field of battle than Crocker. With his cheek bone crushed and his ear shot off, he urged his men to advance, shouting, "We'll lick them all yet!"

After the battle, the 11th, 13th, 15th, and 16th Iowa regiments were regrouped under the leadership of Crocker, who now bore a new title: brigadier-general. The new regiment was named the Crocker Brigade. The Crocker Brigade was to fight through to the end of the war and become the only group in the army of the Union to hold its original organization to the end.

Crocker and his Brigade fought on with General Grant in his Campaign of the West: at Jackson, at Champion Hills, and in the attack on Vicksburg. General Grant could find no regiment better trained than the famous Iowa Crocker Brigade. The regiment became known for its soldierly discipline, promptness of movement in battle and gallantry under fire. No regiment had cleaner camps, no regiment kept their arms in such excellent repair, and no men were braver when the cannon balls tore into their ranks. The history of the Crocker Brigade became the history of the Civil War.

One night when Crocker was tenting near General Grant, the General became disturbed over the consistent coughing which came from the next tent. The next morning Grant called Crocker to him and said, "General Crocker, was that you coughing so last night?"

Crocker, fearing that he had disturbed the sleep of the commander, answered reluctantly, "Yes, General."

"Well, my dear fellow," ordered Grant, "you must go straight home, for you'll die here."

Few people knew that when the fiery young lawyer had leaped upon his chair at the meeting hall in Des Moines that he was very near to becoming an invalid from the dread disease of tuberculosis. His health did not stop the fighting Crocker. General Grant wrote of him in his *Memoirs*, "Crocker, however, was dying of consumption when he volunteered. His weak condition never put him on the sick report when there was a battle in prospect as long as he could keep on his feet."

Finally in 1863, there was no choice left for the brave Crocker but to come north to rest and recuperate. He returned to Des Moines for a short time, and then hurriedly joined his brigade to accompany General Sherman on his March to the Sea.

Crocker Resigns

As Sherman's army plunged on through north Alabama and northwest Georgia, preparing to enter Atlanta, General Crocker finally found himself so weak physically that he was unable to keep up. He knew that he would have to go home. Only a few of his officers knew of his decision. As the gallant Iowa brigade swung down the road, General Crocker, mounted on his favorite horse "Beauregard" pulled at the reins and steered the animal to the rear of the advancing column. The regiment broke out in a cheer as he passed. As he continued his lonely ride back to Des Moines, the cheers of his men and the sounds of battle reechoed in his mind: Shiloh, Corinth, Bolivar, Raymond, Jackson, Champion Hill, Vicksburg. If his health had only been stronger, who knows how many more battles would have been added to the impressive list.

Within a year he was back in the army. He accepted a command in New Mexico, hoping that the mild climate might restore him to health, but he could not stay out of the conflict. He left his post in New Mexico and started back to rejoin his brigade. He traveled as far as Washington, D.C., where he died in a hotel.

Crocker Brigade Marches On

The Crocker Brigade went on without its battling leader. They took part in the siege of Atlanta and pounded on to the sea. They reached Alexandria, Virginia, on May 19th, where they remained until the grand review was held in Washington at the close of the war.

"Crocker's Iowa Brigade will ever hold a place in the history of the Civil War," said General Sherman. General Grant added his praise for the Iowa volunteers, "It is a brigade renowned for its marches, its battles, its losses, and for the high soldierly qualities of its first commander."

The Crocker Brigade was but one of the many Iowa regiments who fought from Missouri to Virginia. The "immortal First Iowa" in their ragged, cheap uniforms were the vital force in saving southern Missouri from the Rebel forces. It was Grenville Mellen Dodge of Council Bluffs, one of Iowa's four major-generals, who built a bridge 14 feet high and 710 feet long across the Chattahoochee River in three days. His engineering ability was an important factor in General Grant's successful campaign in the west.

It was an Iowa regiment that crossed the river in an old flat boat and hoisted their Iowa regiment flag over

Soldiers and Sailors Monument on the Capitol Grounds

Columbia, South Carolina, the spot where the first banner of the secession had flown.

Two-thirds of the male population of military age in Iowa were engaged in the fighting during the Civil War. One-fifth of this number lost their lives. Many of these volunteers actually marched from the Des Moines River, through the South, and on to Richmond. Some traveled

222

10,000 miles on foot and a few the distance equal to a trip around the world.

The nation did not forget Iowa's battling young lawyer from Des Moines. In Military Park at Vicksburg is a large pedestal bust of General Marcellus Monroe Crocker.

Nor did Iowa forget its brave soldier. On the capitol grounds in Des Moines stands a tall monument dedicated to the soldiers and sailors of the Civil War. A prominent part of the monument is occupied by a statue of Crocker astride "Beauregard".

A school, a street, a park, a railroad station in Des Moines were all named for the invincible Crocker. Marking his grave in a Des Moines cemetery is a stone engraved with the words of General Grant: "General Crocker was fit to command an independent army."

UNIT VI

Iowa Grows

In America today, automobiles, buses, planes, telephones, radio, television, and such means of transportation and communication are commonplace. The great change that made this possible took place after the Civil War.

The United States entered a period of growth and expansion. Almost overnight America went from a farming to an industrial nation. Giant industry developed with breathtaking speed. This development took place all over the nation. The South found ways of salvaging its agriculture and at the same time started building factories. In the Midwest, industry developed around agricultural products. Flour mills, cereal processing, and meat packing caused the growth of midwestern cities.

The West was settled rapidly. Discovery of ore deposits plus a generous land policy by the Government caused the West to be soon dotted with mining towns and cattle ranches. By 1890 the President declared that the frontier no longer existed.

The railroads were the key to both the growth of industry and the settlement of the West. Five transcontinental railroads were built. The railroad, more than any one single thing, tied the country together. It not only transported manufactured goods and farm produce, it also served a social purpose. People in cities and rural areas began to understand each other better. The result of this period of growth was a new unity and a better and stronger America.

Chapter 21

KATE SAVES THE EXPRESS

"Get in the wash, Kate. There's another blow heading this way," shouted Mother Shelley as she ran to shut up the chickens.

It *was* another blow. The clouds gathering in the southwest were churning and black. By the time Kate had pulled the clean clothes from the line and scampered up on the porch, big drops of rain were pelting down. Kate stood on the porch and watched the rain sweep down across the little valley.

It was July of 1881. Never had the citizens of Moingona seen such a spring and summer. Storms and torrential rains had caused Honey Creek and the big Des Moines River to run bankful for weeks.

The Shelley family lived in a little cottage perched on the side of Honey Creek Valley beside the Chicago and North Western Railroad about a half a mile from the Des Moines River. Just up the valley was a railroad bridge across Honey Creek. The railroad track curved down through the valley, crossed a high wooden trestle that spanned the wide Des Moines River, and wound around into the little railroad town of Moingona in central Iowa.

Kate's father, an immigrant from Tipperary, Ireland, had been one of the many workers who had come over to America to help in the building of the railroads that were fanning out over all of Iowa in the middle and late 1800's. For many years, until his death three years before, Mr. Shelley had been a section foreman for the railroad company. He had seen the railroads grow in the years that he had made Iowa his home.

Coming of the Railroad

The railroad had first come to Iowa in 1856. The first train whistled around the bend into Iowa City from Davenport one cold January morning with the temperature standing at 18 degrees below zero. The citizens in Davenport and Iowa City had been promised that a railroad line, linking the two towns, would be completed by New Year's Day. To help finish the track on time, settlers along the route had turned out to help lay the last ties and pound the spikes. They built huge bonfires along the tracks to keep the workers warm and to provide light as the men worked through the long winter night. A locomotive, the "Antoine Le Claire"[1] had been ferried across the Mississippi River on a flat boat to pull the first train. There was no bridge across the river into Iowa at this time.

The happy citizens prepared an elaborate celebration. In spite of the cold weather, they met the train about a mile and a half out and followed it into the city. When the "Muscatine", pulled by the "Antoine Le

[1] Antoine Le Claire was an early fur trader and interpreter. He has often been called the "father of Davenport." Le Claire broke the first ground for the railroad line.

Claire" chugged into the capital city with its load of rail-road and state dignitaries, the citizens fired a cannon and the celebration began. It was a great day in Iowa history.

For many years Iowa had depended upon the great natural highway of trade—the rivers. At one time Du-buque had as many as 11 boats leaving daily. Horse ferries carried the early settlers across the Mississippi into Iowa, and when the river froze, sleighs were built that could be pulled across. They were so constructed that if the ice gave away, the sleighs would float. The smaller rivers inside Iowa were too shallow for steam-boat traffic. Within Iowa, horse and stagecoach routes provided the transportation.

When the railroads began to appear on the eastern shore of the Mississippi, eager Iowa settlers caught the railroad fever. Iowa's rich farm soil demanded a system of railroads to carry the produce to the eastern markets. At first the settlers paid out of their own savings to buy stock in railroad companies in order that Iowa could have railway transportation too. Iowans, however, had not accumulated enough money to pay the complete cost of building, so Congress made free grants of land to the railroad companies. Every other section of land for six miles on either side of a proposed railroad line was given to the new company. This was equal to a strip of land 24 miles wide across the state.

By 1873 Iowa formed a link in the great railroad lines that crossed the continent from the Atlantic Ocean to the Pacific. Iowa was bustling with railroad building. Little towns sprung up throughout the state wherever the railroad line came through. Kate was proud of the part her father had played in bringing the railroad to Iowa.

A Flood at Midnight

As the storm broke over the Little Honey Creek Valley that July afternoon, Mother Shelley and her children watched in alarm. Honey Creek was soon a raging torrent, and the water had begun to creep up to the little hillside farm. Kate, fifteen years old and the oldest of the children, went out into the storm to let the cows and horses out of the barn which was already filling with water. As she hurried back to the house, she wondered if the long wooden trestle bridge across the Des Moines River could possibly withstand the flooding water which was now sweeping past, carrying fence posts and uprooted trees.

About midnight, the younger children having dropped off to sleep, Kate and her mother heard the whistle of the pusher engine in the distance and then the rumble as it crossed the Des Moines River trestle. The pusher was an engine that was kept at Moingona to help the heavy freight and passenger trains up the hill on each side of the valley. It had been ordered to go from Moingona to Boonesboro to look for any possible washouts. Between the flashes of lightning, Kate and her mother watched the little engine as it passed by and moved on to the swaying bridge over Honey Creek. The engine's bell rang out bravely between the claps of thunder. Suddenly there was a loud crash, a hissing of steam as the engine hit the water, and then only a strange silence in the lull of the storm.

"They've gone down!" screamed Kate.

"And the midnight express from the west is due any minute," cried Mother Shelley.

The young girl knew that she must go to help the men on the pusher engine and that in some way she must try to stop the passenger train that would soon be coming through to Moingona.

"I'm going to help," cried Kate, as she grabbed an old miner's lantern.

All the valley was now flooded, even the front yard of the Shelley home. Kate had to turn back and go behind the house and follow the crest of the hill around to where a wagon road came in through a bluff and crossed the railroad. She followed the track to the broken bridge. Two men had climbed out of the wrecked engine and were clinging to the branch of a tree. There was no trace of the other two crew members.

She saw at once that she could not rescue the men in the flood, but must go for help. Most important of all she must stop the passenger train before it, too, plunged through the broken bridge. Moingona was a mile and a quarter away, but between was the long high wooden trestle bridge, now swaying and trembling over the flooded Des Moines.

She would have to cross the trestle. What if the train were to come while she was crossing? What if the old wood trestle were to collapse from the flood-weakened embankments as she crossed? What if the passenger train did not see her in the darkness and roared past her?

When she reached the trestle, she saw that the flood waters were almost level with the track. The storm broke out again with even more fierceness. The wind almost blew her off her feet as she started across the trestle.

The railroad company had purposely built the bridge so that children would not attempt to cross it. They had removed the planking and had set the ties so far apart that a child could not step from tie to tie except with great difficulty. Rusty spikes projected from the slippery, rain-soaked track, but Kate Shelley went on. A sudden gust of wind caught her and blew out her lantern. Now she was in complete darkness. She got down on her hands and knees and crawled slowly along. Her skirt caught on the spikes and threw her off balance, but on she went. The spikes cut into her hands and knees. About halfway across a flash of lightning showed a full grown tree, its roots full of tons of dirt, bearing down upon the trestle. Surely the old wooden frame of the bridge could not withstand the force when this hit the supports. She stood upright on her knees, but just at the last instant, the tree twisted, turned, and threaded its way between the support posts and surged under the bridge with an angry hiss.

The bridge seemed endless. At times Kate thought that the other side was getting farther away instead of closer. At last she felt the solid ground of the other shore beneath her feet, but she still had a quarter of a mile to go along the track. She caught her breath for a moment and then began to run down the track as it curved into Moingona.

The Moingona station agent had just stepped out of the depot with his lantern to check the progress of the storm when he saw the wild-looking child running up the track toward him.

"Honey Creek Bridge's out! Stop the train!" Kate gasped.

"Why it's the Shelley girl," he cried. "You mean you crossed the trestle in this storm?"

"The pusher crew's down in Honey Creek . . . hanging on to a tree. You've got to help them!" screamed the girl.

The message to stop the passenger train was wired ahead. An engine whistle summoned the citizens of the

The old depot at Moingona

little railroad town for the emergency. A rescue party gathered with ropes and rescue equipment.

After a brief rest, Kate guided the men along the bluffs back to the point where the two men of the pusher crew were still hanging on to the tree branch. A rope was thrown to one of them. He fastened it to the tree and crawled, hand over hand, to safety. The other man had to wait until the storm was over before the rescue party could reach him.

Kate Is Rewarded

During the days that followed, 15-year old Kate Shelley became a world wide heroine. News of her heroism was flashed around the world; and poems, editorials, and readings were written about her. The Iowa State Legislature presented her with a gold medal and $200 in cash. The employees of the railroad gave her a gold watch and chain and issued her a life pass on the railroad. Trains passing the Shelley home were given per-

The Kate Shelley Bridge near Moingona

mission to stop in the middle of Honey Creek Valley for Kate if she wished to board the train.

When Kate was older, she became the station agent at Moingona. A steel bridge was erected over the Des Moines River to replace the old wooden trestle. The new bridge was named the Kate Shelley Bridge in memory of her brave act that July night.

At one time Iowa could boast that there was no spot in the state that was farther than 12 miles from a railroad line, but with the coming of the automobile and the airplane, the railroads began to decline. As a result, small Iowa towns dwindled and many died out completely. Today all that is left of the monument to Kate Shelley are two huge stone piers on each side of the Des Moines River and a deserted railroad embankment leading to Moingona, but the story of Kate Shelley is remembered throughout Iowa as a chapter in the history of railroading.

Chapter 22

SCHOOLMASTER JENNINGS

The young schoolmaster rapped on his desk for order one October morning in 1830 and the first school in Iowa opened.

Mr. Berryman Jennings, a polished young gentleman of twenty-three, looked over his eight pupils assembled in the little log cabin. There were the Galland children—Washington, David, and Eliza—and the two Dedmans—Tolliver and James—and three of the other neighboring children of the pioneer settlement. The new schoolmaster could tell at a glance that he must show no "hesitancy in applying the rod" if he were to keep order. Already he had singled out a 16-year old bully that he would have to discipline. They would start with the ABC's this first morning, Mr. Jennings decided, and then move on to writing, and perhaps attempt some "ciphering".

Dr. Isaac Galland had moved his family westward across the Mississippi in 1829 into the Half Breed Reservation, that tract of land that juts downward like a thumb from the southeast corner of the present state of

Iowa. The land had been set aside for the children of mixed white and Indian parents. Most of the half breeds that lived there were traders, trappers, or interpreters. The land had not yet been opened for white settlement; in fact, it had not even been given a name when the Gallands moved in.

The doctor was a scholarly man, well-educated in literature and medicine. Later he wrote a book on Iowa called *Iowa Emigrant,* that gave useful information about the new territory and influenced many pioneers to come to Iowa. Like most of the early pioneers, he had started to think about a school for his children as soon as he had his log cabin built and the prairie sod broken.

The First Schoolhouse

Dr. Galland built the schoolhouse himself, hewing down the round logs, notching them to fit, and filling in the cracks with mud. The schoolhouse was small, 10' by 12', with a fireplace at one end. The floor was split logs. There were only two windows, one on each side

The replica of the old Galland schoolhouse near Keokuk

235

wall, covered with greased paper. Split logs grooved into the wall made desks and benches for the pupils. The children fashioned their own pens from goose quills, and Mrs. Galland mixed up some homemade ink. The only books the children had from which to study were those they could find at home. As Dr. Galland wrote in his book in comparing the Iowa school with those in other parts of the United States: "If they have better schools, they have no better scholars."

After the doctor had the schoolhouse built, he went back across the Mississippi that summer in 1830 and met Berryman Jennings, a sprightly young Kentuckian. Berryman Jennings impressed the doctor as a young man who was educated "beyond his fellows." Would he come to Ahwipetuk, as the Indians called the settlement at the head of the rapids where Galland had settled, and teach in the new school? Dr. Galland would give him his board, room and allow him to study in his books on medicine. The school would be open only during the months of October, November and December. Young Jennings had agreed, and here he was the first and only schoolmaster in the vast new region that stretched north of Missouri and west of the Mississippi River.

The first school in Iowa operated only one term. During the young schoolmaster's term, an event took place in the Galland household that was most historic. The Gallands had a new baby, Eleanor. She was the first white child born in what is now Iowa. Before another term of school could begin, the young schoolteacher became ill and was forced to return to his home in Warsaw, Illinois.

"Build a church and raise a school"

Other white settlements west of the Mississippi soon

followed Dr. Galland's example. A school was started in Keokuk, then called Puckeshetuk. The school was taught by Mr. I. K. Robinson during the months of December of 1830 and January and February of 1831.

The first school held outside the Half Breed Tract was started three years later at Dubuque and was taught by George Cubbage. The story is told that this unfortunate schoolmaster was captured one day by a tribe of warlike Indians. The savages tore off his coonskin cap, intending to scalp the poor man, but to their astonishment they found that Schoolmaster Cubbage was bald. How could an Indian warrior scalp a bald school teacher? Disgustedly the Indians traded him for some tobacco, and Mr. Cubbage lived to return to his schoolmaster's desk to teach again.

"Build a church and raise a school" soon became the aim of every little pioneer settlement in Iowa. By the time the land had become a territory, five years later, there were more than forty schools, but they were mostly private schools run by persons who accepted children that were sent to them. Often the teacher would go from cabin to cabin teaching the children in their own homes. The teacher would give them lessons that he had copied on paper and return the next day to hear the lessons. The pupils had to figure their arithmetic problems in their heads. The early teachers said that this was fine training for their minds, and, furthermore, it saved paper, which was scarce in pioneer times.

Governor Lucas in his first message to his Territorial Legislature said, "There is no subject to which I wish to call your attention more emphatically than the subject of establishing a well planned system of common schools."

A one-room schoolhouse

The One-Room Country School

As Iowa assumed statehood and the prairies were cut
up into farm homesteads, a little white frame schoolhouse appeared in the middle of each four sections of
land. The early lawmakers reasoned that no child should
have to walk more than two miles to school.

Usually all eight grades were taught by a single
teacher, who boarded around at the various homes as
part payment of his salary. School was in session only
during the winter months when the farm work on the
new homesteads did not demand the children's help.
Often the pupils were well in their twenties before they
finished eight grades of school. One such farm lad, who
had been able to attend just a few months each year,
was 21 years old and had been elected the director of
the school while he was still in the eighth grade. One
day, when the young man had done something which

the schoolmaster did not like, he was placed in the front seat for punishment. This caused much merriment among the other pupils to see the school director sitting in the front row.

The one-room schoolhouse was usually set in the center of an acre plot of land. A coal stove furnished the heat, with the teacher acting as fireman and janitor. The salary of the schoolteacher was often no more than $25 a month and was often paid in farm produce. Much of the teaching was done through memory work. The teacher would take the history book and say, "Shall we begin?" The pupil would begin to recite the entire history chapter from memory.

On Friday afternoon the pupils would be divided into two sides and stand on each side of the room and hold a spelling bee. Each pupil, upon misspelling a word, would sit down until only one was left standing, the champion speller. Arithmetic was worked on blackboards, planks painted black, or on small individual slates.

The little one-room schoolhouse has all but disappeared from Iowa today, and modern elementary buildings located in neighboring towns have replaced them.

Iowa High Schools and Universities

At first the laws of the new state were only interested in grade schools. Not more than ten years after Iowa became a state, the first high school was started in Tipton in Cedar County. It was called the Tipton Union School. Iowa high schools had to wait until after the Civil War to become firmly established in Iowa education. From the end of the War on, more than 950 high schools developed in Iowa, averaging nearly nine high schools for each county. There were as many high schools as there

The Campanile on the campus of Iowa State University at Ames

were cities and towns in Iowa besides the many consolidated high schools which sprang up in the open country. In 1911 a law was passed making high schools free to every child in Iowa.

Since World War II Iowans have taken a second look at their schools. Did the quantity of the schools guarantee the quality of the schools, particularly when the schools were very small? Reorganization of small high schools into larger districts began. Instead of boasting about nine small high schools in every county, the

Salisbury House in Des Moines, headquarters of the Iowa State Education Association

people of Iowa began to think about one or two large high schools in each county.

Iowans have always been proud of the number of its people that are able to read and write—about 99.2% of the entire population at the present time. Since the time when the Old Stone Capitol was converted into the hub of the University of Iowa campus in 1856, Iowa has shown a great interest in its colleges and universities. Three state schools are supported by the taxes of the Iowa people: the State University of Iowa at Iowa City, Iowa State University at Ames, and the University of Northern Iowa at Cedar Falls.

Some colleges were started before Iowa became a state. Loras College in Dubuque was founded in 1838 by the Catholic Church. The Methodists founded Iowa

241

Wesleyan College in 1843 at Mount Pleasant, and Grinnell was founded in 1846 by a group of young missionaries of the Congregational and Presbyterian churches. Today various religious groups maintain more than 22 schools of higher education. Besides the state and church supported colleges, Iowa has 23 junior colleges.

According to Iowa law, a child must attend school until he is sixteen years old or until he has graduated from the eighth grade. If he wishes to continue through high school and college, Iowa offers ample opportunity for him to do so. The education of Iowa is controlled at the state level by the Superintendent of Public Instruction, at the county level by a County Superintendent, and at the local level by an elected school board.

The tiny Galland school has long disappeared under the Keokuk Dam, which was built on the Des Moines Rapids in the Mississippi River, but on the bank of the Mississippi, just below Montrose, the state of Iowa has erected an exact replica of Iowa's first school. Here modern Iowans may see how their great educational system first began under the stern direction of the young schoolmaster, Berryman Jennings.

Chapter 23

A CHURCH IN THE VALE

Barton Randle rode into Dubuque one November day in 1833, his possessions in his saddle bag and his Bible in his hand.

Randle had been sent to Dubuque to preach the Word of God. There was no church in which to preach; in fact, there was almost no town. Beside the lead mines were a few log cabins and shanties built along a shapeless street, a grocery store, and a tavern. It did not look a promising place for a preacher.

The Reverend Randle was not easily discouraged. He had been sent by the Methodist Church to preach, and he would find a place. That evening he held his first church service in the local tavern.*

Religion had come to Iowa as early as 1673 when Marquette and Joliet had paddled their way down the Mississippi. Marquette had told the Sac and Fox Indians about the Christian religion. Following that, Catholic priests had been missionaries to the Indians for many

---

* A public house where guests could receive food, lodging and drink.

years before there were any white settlements, but the first church in Iowa was built by the Methodists.

Preaching a church service in a tavern had its drawbacks. Among other things, it was not a very suitable place for a minister to stay. Barton Randle found another place to hold his services——over the grocery store. This did not prove any more satisfactory. It was a combined grocery store and saloon. So much quarreling and fighting went on it was nearly impossible to conduct a church service.

Plans soon got under way to build a suitable church. Seventy people donated funds ranging from 12c to $25. Of the ones who donated, only three or four belonged to the Methodist Church. Everybody in the community helped build the church, including the gamblers. Made of hewn logs, it was twenty feet wide, twenty six feet long, and cost $250. Membership included twelve persons, five men and seven women. Barton Randle's wages were $100 for the one year he preached in Dubuque.

At the time the church was built it was understood that although it was a Methodist Church, anyone could use it. One day a Mormon missionary came to Dubuque and wanted to use the church. It was whispered around that the Methodists had locked the church and would not let the man in to preach. A young man elbowed his way through the crowd that had gathered and stuck his knife in the door of the church. The crowd took up the chant, and the Mormon was allowed to go inside and preach his sermon.

It was also understood at the time of the building of the church that it could be used for community gatherings. Through the years it was used for a school and then for the hearings of court trials.

Although most early settlements were not fortunate

enough to have a church, by 1838 there were a number of churches in Iowa. Where there were no churches, people had to adjust their religion to the influence of the frontier. Settlements were scattered and the pastors had to take the church to the people. The circuit rider, the camp meeting, and the revival became the religious way of life among the Presbyterian, Baptist, and Methodist churches. People would come with their tents and enough provisions to last a week. Social as well as spiritual revival came with the sermons, Bible reading, and hymn singing.

Of all the denominations, the organization of the Methodist Church seemed best suited to the frontier. As new settlements developed, the Bishop would send out a traveling preacher. These ministers were given a fixed circuit, going from one settlement to another on horseback or afoot. The Reverend Barton Randle was only one of many who followed the settlers into Iowa and worked among them for almost no pay. Most of these early preachers died early from overwork and overexposure. They walked or rode across the prairies, wading the streams, facing the heat of summer and the blizzards of winter. The labor was great and the financial rewards were few. But if these preachers went hungry, so did the people whom they served. And whatever they had to share, they shared generously.

One of these early preachers was Barton Cartwright who broke sod for a living, for he received no pay as a minister. He organized the first Methodist Society in Burlington in 1834. Three years later this group began to build a brick church that came to be known as "Old Zion". Old Zion was used as the capitol building of the Wisconsin Territory when Burlington was the capital. The building they had been using had burned down.

When the Territory of Iowa was created in 1837, the first three sessions of the Iowa Legislature met in Old Zion. Governor Robert Lucas held a Council with the Sac and Fox Indians there in 1840. When the Territorial government was moved to Iowa City in 1841, Old Zion once again became a church.

Battle of the Bell

The first church west of the Mississippi to have a bell was the Presbyterian Church in Iowa City. It was the pride of the members and the envy of the other congregations to have the bell call the Presbyterians to worship each Sunday morning. Fortunate as they were to have a bell, they were not so fortunate in their choice of a minister. The Reverend Hummer became very unpopular with his congregation, was expelled from the ministry in 1848 and asked to leave town. His salary had not been paid, so he secured the right to take movable property from the church as part payment on his salary.

The Reverend Hummer decided this included the bell. A crowd gathered to watch while he lowered the bell to the ground and into the wagon. While he was still in the belfry, someone removed the ladder, leaving him imprisoned in the belfry. He watched helplessly as the culprits drove off with the bell. Not knowing what to do with the bell after they had taken it, the pranksters sunk it in the Iowa River at the mouth of Rapid Creek. Later they went back to get it and found it missing. Years later it was learned that two Mormons on their way to Utah took the bell with them and sold it to Brigham Young.

The Catholic Church in Iowa

Several Catholic priests had visited the Half Breed Tract long before territorial days, and no doubt the simple services they conducted were the first religious ceremonies of Iowaland. But it was not until a year after Barton Randle had built his Methodist Church in Dubuque that the first Catholic Church was built in the same settlement.

A few years later an abbot from Ireland with four Trappist brothers founded a monastery twelve miles from Dubuque. The Trappists had originally located in France, but during the reign of Napoleon, they had been forced to flee to Ireland. When Mount Melleray Abbey in Ireland became too crowded, the Trappists looked to America. In 1849, Bishop Mathias Loras, of the See of Dubuque, offered these monks some land on which to establish an order.

Today, amid a cluster of pine trees, can be seen the massive abbey of limestone—the Abbey of Our Lady of New Melleray. There, about one hundred thirty monks live a simple life of prayer, working in their gardens and on their farm, talking only when it is absolutely necessary. The monks rise early, two o'clock in the morning, and go to bed at seven in the evening. They cut their hair short and let their beards grow. They wear the ancient costume of a long, brown, woolen robe with a hood and leather girdle.

Near Festina, twelve miles from Decorah, in northeast Iowa, is the tiny St. Anthony of Padua Chapel, the smallest cathedral in the world. The tiny church was built by Johann Gaertner and seats only eight people. Johann was a soldier under Napoleon and took part in the famed march on Russia. His mother prayed that his life might be spared and promised to build a chapel if her prayers were answered. Johann survived, but his mother died before she could carry out her promise. Johann came to America in 1840 and settled near Fes-

St. Anthony's Chapel near Festina

tina. When the Catholic Church in the little settlement burned, Gaertner carried out his mother's wishes and built the tiny chapel for the family worship.

Another Catholic Church which has long attracted world-wide attention is the Grotto of the Redemption at West Bend in Palo Alto County. This unique construction was built by Father Dobberstein in his spare time from materials gathered from all over the world. Besides

248

Grotto of the Redemption at West Bend

its art value, the grotto contains one of the most complete geological collections in the United States.

Perhaps the best known Catholic priest in Iowa history was Father Samuel Mazzuchelli, who came from Italy in 1828 and worked among the Indians and half breeds of eastern Iowa. Traveling by horse or by foot, Father Mazzuchelli ministered to his parish which included most of the upper Mississippi Valley. Besides being a dedicated priest, Father Mazzuchelli was a noted architect. Several of the early churches of his faith in eastern Iowa were designed by him, and many think he was responsible for the architecture of the Old Stone Capitol at Iowa City.

As pioneer settlements spread westward across the state, so did the Church. Although the Iowa pioneer was stern and unbending in his belief, he often balanced this with tolerance toward those whose belief was different. Thus, religion in Iowa came to be found in many shapes and forms. As city living became more and more a part of Iowa, the spires of great cathedrals began reaching toward the sky. The rural church at the crossroads became less and less a part of the Iowa scene. Today many of these churches remain only as monuments on the prairie to the faith of the pioneers.

The Little Brown Church

As Iowa faces the future, she clings to the past. In religion, the people have made a shrine of a little church painted brown that seems to embody this simplicity of faith. Severe in its plainness, quiet in its brown exterior, the Little Brown Church at Nashua reflects a dignity in its wooded setting that no cathedral could ever capture.

In 1857, Dr. William Pitts visited the village of Bradford near Charles City. He was impressed by the beauty of the valley. Near the close of the day, just as the sun was going down behind the trees along the Cedar River, he came upon a spot where it seemed to him a church should be. After going back to Wisconsin, he wrote the words and music to "The Little Brown Church In The Vale". He made no use of the hymn in Wisconsin, but when he came to Fredericksburg in 1862, he brought the song with him. In the winter of 1864 he went to Bradford to teach a singing class. He discovered that a church had been built on the very spot where he had envisioned it. Taking his singing class, which included the Reverend Nutting, to the unfinished church, they improvised pews out of boards. There Dr. Pitts sang "The Little Brown Church In The Vale" for the first time in public.

In the spring of 1865 the church was dedicated just

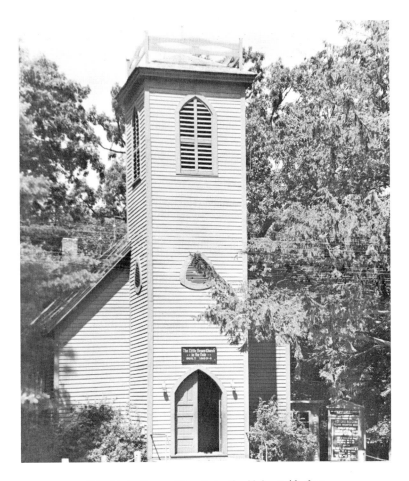

The Little Brown Church in the Vale at Nashua

about the time the song was published. Several months before the song was published, the church had been painted brown. Whether it was because brown paint was cheaper then, or whether it was a desire to conform to the words of the song, it is not known, but the little church is exactly the right color as it mushrooms from the earth among the protecting grove of oak and pine.

As thousands of people each year make a pilgrimage

251

to the Little Brown Church and as hundreds of young couples each year say their marriage vows at its altar, the Little Brown Church links the heritage of the past with the hope of the future.

UNIT VII

Two Wars and a Depression

By 1900 the United States had become a powerful country. After a war with Spain, the United States began to get interested in the affairs of the world and acquired possessions beyond its borders. Some of these were Puerto Rico, Hawaii and the Phillipines.

The United States took part in World War I, but when it was over it did not join the League of Nations. Isolationism, a part of her foreign policy for many years, returned.

World-wide depression followed World War I, and the United States suffered from it as well as the rest of the world. While America solved her problems in a democratic way, the rest of the world was not so fortunate. Dictatorships rose in Italy, Germany, and Japan and brought on World War II.

Attacked by Japan at Pearl Harbor on December 7, 1941, the United States placed her military strength with her allies, and victory was won.

As the war was drawing to a close, the United States made plans for a world organization designed to keep peace. In 1945 at San Francisco, delegates from fifty nations met and drew up the charter for the United Nations.

Chapter 24

MERLE HAY—LOST IN ACTION

In western Iowa, where the prairie begins to flatten out into the plains, lies the little Carroll County town of Glidden. Forced into being by the farmers' need for a grain elevator and a railway station, it looks very much like any western Iowa town. Age has added a graceful beauty to the oaks, the elms, and the maples that arch over the streets. The REA* building on the north side of the busy highway has brought a modern touch. But there is nothing about Glidden that would let anyone know that a moment in time had pinpointed it to be forever marked by history.

His boyhood

Into this thriving farm community, Merle Hay was born on July 30, 1896. His childhood and period of youth were shaped and molded by the rural activities a farm boy would experience. Along with his brother and sister he performed, sometimes with protest, the tasks

* Rural Electrification Association.

254

given to farm boys and girls. Chasing the disapproving chickens from the nest, he gathered the eggs. Feeling the dewy dampness of the cool grass on his bare feet, he took the cows out to pasture after the morning milking. In the humid heat of an Iowa summer day, he helped hoe the morning glories out of the rapidly-growing corn.

Sometimes the pull of the Raccoon River proved to be too much for Merle and his brother. Slipping away from the sticky, dusty heat of the hayfield, they would take forbidden dips in the cool water under the shade of a cottonwood tree.

Secure in the comfort and love of the family home, Merle Hay grew to manhood. War clouds were gathering and had broken over Europe by the time he reached his eighteenth birthday. But Europe was far away from America in 1914. As Merle Hay completed his schooling and took jobs on neighboring farms, the thought of war was as far away as Europe itself.

Despite the distance, the war kept coming closer to the United States. As German submarines continued to sink American ships, the American attitude changed. On April 6, 1917, the United States entered World War I against Germany.

His enlistment

Merle Hay was one of the eight young men from the Glidden community who enlisted shortly after the United States entered the war. On May 3, 1917, he went to Des Moines and enlisted in the Coast Artillery. The events that followed happened with startling swiftness. By May 20th the young soldiers were at Fort Bliss, Texas. They had no way of knowing that even as they were getting settled in their barracks at Fort Bliss, a telegram had arrived from the War Department, ordering the formation of a First Division to be sent overseas to France. Merle Hay and the others who had volunteered for the Coast Artillery found themselves a part of the 16th Infantry of this First Division. The war had suddenly become very close.

A month from the day Merle Hay had enlisted, the 16th Infantry left Fort Bliss by railway for Hoboken, New Jersey, where troopships were being readied for the journey across the ocean. On the morning of June 14th, as naval vessels hovered alongside, the troopships slid out to sea. Less than two weeks later they were in France.

Spending the next few months in training camps, Merle Hay was a homesick, lonesome young man. His twenty-first birthday was on July thirtieth. That day he wrote on the flyleaf of his Bible, "Twenty-one years old today—someplace in France."

The movement toward the trenches began on the twentieth of October. Rain had been falling all of that day and for many days before. Marching along in the rain, sloshing through the water-filled tracks, the inexperienced American soldiers made their way to the front lines.

The trenches were as filled with mud and water as the road on which they had come. These cold, muddy slits in the ground offered little except protection. Before them were the entangled masses of barbed wire and beyond that, the Germans.

His Death

In the cold, cheerless dawn of November 3, a German raid began. Concentrating their fire upon the portion of the trench occupied by the Americans, they managed to isolate a small detachment from the main body. Crawling over the muddy ground through the darkness, the Germans jumped into the trench. A handful of American troops, cut from the main section, engaged in hand to hand fighting against overwhelming odds. When the fighting was over, Merle Hay and two of his companions were dead.

America was suddenly shocked into the realization that it was no longer playing at war. Whatever glamour this first World War might have had ended abruptly that gray November day as the telegram from the War Department arrived at the Harvey Hay farm home at Glidden.

It read:

Deeply regret to inform you that Private Merle D. Hay, Company F, 16th Infantry, is reported killed in action.

As the Hay family learned of their son's death, the state learned of the significance of his death. To Merle Hay goes, and will always belong, the glory of representing Iowa's soldiers killed in battle in World War I. He was the first Iowa soldier and one of the first three Americans killed.

In the little town of Glidden, flags flew at half mast that day. Caught up in the tragedy of this event, people huddled in little groups and talked in subdued tones about the swiftness with which death had come to this boy. The chances were about one in one hundred thousand that the first blow of the war would fall upon Glidden. And yet coupled with this feeling of tragedy was one of honor and pride that this boy's life should be the first one offered up in the cause of freedom.

As Glidden prepared for a memorial service, other action was taking place around the state. A representative to the state legislature from Clinton suggested that Merle Hay's birthday be a patriotic holiday in Iowa. Meeting in Des Moines, the City Council announced the naming of the road connecting the city with Camp Dodge "to be hereinafter known 'as Merle Hay Road." Speaking for the Council, the Mayor said, "I feel it would be appropriate to have a road leading to the camp where soldiers are trained to take their places in the field against the enemy, bear the name of the first of our soldiers to be killed in action."

The three American soldiers were buried in France. Over their grave the French government erected a monument with this inscription:

"Here lies the first soldiers of the Republic of the United States to fall on the soil of France for liberty and justice."

On February 7, 1918, Harvey D. Hay received from the colonel of the 16th Infantry the French Croix de Guerre* which was awarded by the Republic of France to Merle Hay at the time of his death.

Three years later, July, 1921, Merle Hay's body was taken from its resting place in the soil of France and was brought home for burial. Ten thousand people came to Glidden that Sunday afternoon to honor the state's greatest war hero. There had been considerable discussion around the state about putting up a monument, but at the time of the burial the only marker was an inconspicuous headstone placed there by his family.

Fame, even to those who have died a hero's death, is often a fleeting thing. Merle Hay's body continued to lie in the Glidden cemetery with no further mention of a memorial. Along the south side of the cemetery runs one of the nation's great highways, Highway 30. Day

*A French medal awarded for gallant action in war.

The Merle Hay Memorial on Highway 30 near Glidden

by day the cars whizzed by in ever-increasing numbers. If anyone had chanced to stop at the little cemetery along the side of the road, no one would have guessed that a state's hero lay beneath its sod.

They would have learned only this:

Merle D. Hay
1896-1917
Company F, 1st Division
16th Infantry

The Monument

Belatedly, in 1930, the State of Iowa erected a monument costing $5000. The money was supplied by the state legislature. The unveiling of the monument on May 29, 1930, again brought thousands of Iowans to honor Merle Hay and other Iowa soldiers who had given their lives in the war. Facing the busy highway, the gray granite memorial carries a reproduction of a cartoon published in the Des Moines Register following Merle Hay's death in 1917. Drawn by Iowa's famous

259

cartoonist, J. N. (Ding) Darling, it shows a sad-faced Uncle Sam with the broken body of an American soldier in his arms.

Since 1930, Iowa and the nation have gone through an even greater world war. Time has dimmed the memories of Merle Hay and what he stood for. It is not too surprising that in 1963 the Polk County Board of Supervisors were talking of changing the name of Merle Hay Road to 58th Street.

Sentiment about Merle Hay may have been slumbering but it was not dead. Protests against the change came quickly, from individuals and from organizations. Merle Hay's name was again in the papers after thirty-three years of little or no recognition. People to whom Merle Hay was only the name of a road and a shopping center in Des Moines learned why his name had been given to the road and why it should always remain there. After considering the protests, the Polk County Board of Supervisors left the name and, for efficiency's sake, added the number 58th Street.

Iowa's Role

That a boy from Iowa was a first American to die in battle in World War I and that he was a farm boy proved to be a symbol of the contribution Iowa was to make to the world.

Coming from every walk of life, 114,000 Iowa men entered the service of their country during World War I. Camp Dodge, near Des Moines, became one of thirty-two training centers in the United States. An all-Iowa Regiment made up the Third Iowa Infantry in the 42nd Division. This 42nd Division became known as the famed Rainbow Division. The Rainbow Division arrived in France in December, 1917. Sent into the trenches in

February, 1918, these soldiers saw some of the heaviest fighting of the war. They stayed at the front until the war ended on November 11, 1918. When the war was over, 3,578 Iowa soldiers had died on the field of battle.

Iowa furnished troops as every state furnished troops. But the starring role Iowa played in the war was in the production of food. The nation and the allies looked to this giant of agriculture to put food into the mouths of the soldiers in the trenches and the starving civilians of Europe. And Iowa came through with what was expected of her.

Herbert Hoover, an Iowan who later became President, became the hero of the war on the civilian front. Over in Europe at the time World War I broke out, he organized the Belgian Relief Commission and saved the Belgians from starving. After the United States entered the war he served as Food Administrator. He urged the farmers to raise as much food as possible and he urged everyone to save food for Europe. He used the slogan, "Food will win the war."

There are two wings flanking the central pillar of the Merle Hay Memorial. On the left, a farmer is toiling in the field to produce food. On the right are soldiers in the heat of battle. Both are giving of their best to the service of their country.

Chapter 25

IOWA BOY BECOMES PRESIDENT

His Boyhood

A chubby, round-faced boy was carefully stepping from one tie to another as he walked down the railroad track. He stood wavering on one bare foot as his eyes searched intently from one side of the graveled railroad bed to the other. Suddenly he stooped down, picked up a stone, dusted it off with a swipe across the side of his overalls, then examined it closely. As though uncertain of what he saw, he licked it with a quick flick of his tongue.

"I think it's an agate," he said to himself, turning the stone over in his hands.

Bending down, he carefully knocked the stone against the railroad track. The chipped corner revealed the bands of color swirling delicately through the stone. A swift feeling of triumph flashed through him.

Stowing the stone carefully away in the side pocket of his overalls, ten year old Bert Hoover started running as fast as his short legs would carry him toward West Branch. He had to show his find to Doc Walker before he left his office.

"What do you have there, boy?" The doctor was turning the key in the door of his office as Bert came puffing and red-faced around the corner with the stone in his hand.

"I'm sure I found an agate. I licked it and it shone like it might be an agate," Bert held the stone out for Dr. Walker to examine.

"Well now, boy, I think you're right." Dr. Walker was turning the stone around and around. "I'd say you had a mighty successful afternoon. When you grow up, Bert, you're going to be a geologist. But you'd better skip along home now or your Uncle Allan and Aunt Millie will have the sheriff out looking for you. It's way past six o'clock."

Flushed with happiness and excitement, Bert ran all the way to his uncle's farm. His chores would be waiting for him. He pumped water into the stock tank for the horses and cows, pulled hay down from the loft and then went to fill the kitchen woodbox for Aunt Millie. He hurried to the woodpile and piled a big load of wood in his arms until it was as high as his nose, and he could just peer over the top. Then he carried it to the woodbox and arranged it in even rows. He was just finishing as his uncle came up from the barn with the pails of milk.

"Uncle Allan, Doc Walker says I found an agate." Bert pulled it out of his pocket and held it in his outstretched hand.

Allan Hoover set the milk pails down and took the stone.

"I don't know anything about stones, Bertie, but I'd

say this is a beauty. You're getting quite a collection. You'll probably sell all these stones some day and be a millionaire." He smiled kindly at his orphaned nephew.

This boy, who was to become the President of the United States, had lived all of his ten years among the gentle Quakers of West Branch. His father and mother were Quakers as their parents and grandparents had been. He was born here on August 10, 1874. His father, Jesse Hoover, was the village blacksmith. His mother was called upon from time to time to act as minister in the Quaker church.

Both of his parents were strong in their faith and thus they taught their children. But Herbert Hoover learned other lessons from his parents: that a day's pay is worthy of a day's work, that strong and healthy minds as well as bodies come from giving children responsibility and proper amounts of work to do. He was taught that simple deeds of kindness bring their own reward.

Bert Hoover's early boyhood days were spent playing with his brother and sister on the grassy lawn that surrounded their two-room cottage. A three-board fence enclosed the lawn. On the top was a flat board, wide enough to walk on. A boy, if he were lucky, could walk all the way around the yard on top of the fence without falling off. The reward was a swing on the white picket gate.

Outside the back door of the cottage was a pump with a tub under the spout and a dipper made from a gourd hanging from a wire hook. Hot dusty children could pump themselves a cool drink and let the rest of the water run into the tub. Washing dirt and dust off bare feet before going to bed was a part of the evening ritual as well as the evening fun.

The blacksmith shop was just north of the cottage. It

Birthplace of Herbert Hoover at West Branch

was fun mingled with fascination for the Hoover children to watch their father at work. As the forge flamed with fiery heat, they watched cautiously from a safe distance just inside the door as the iron turned red hot in the flames. Once Bert stepped on a red hot iron chip with his bare foot. He carried the scar for the rest of his life.

Every day was a day of religion among the Quakers. Along with most of the pioneer groups of Iowa, Bible reading was a daily affair and was considered a part of education. The Hoover children took part in family prayer and Bible reading from a very young age. Sunday service at a Quaker meeting was sometimes a long hour of silence, of waiting for the spirit to move someone to

265

speak. Small Quaker children learned patience and restraint as they sat through this time of silent worship.

This peaceful pace of living marked the first years of Herbert Hoover's life. Sorrow not quite understood came to him at the age of six when his father died of typhoid fever. His mother took in sewing and managed to keep her family together, but three years later she died and the three orphaned children were sent to the homes of relatives.

Herbert Hoover, now nine years old, went to live with his uncle on a farm a mile from West Branch.

Life on a farm was an exciting adventure to Herbert Hoover. His cousin, Walter, was the same age. Together they went fishing for catfish and sunfish with poles cut from a willow tree and string from the butcher shop. In summer they went swimming under the willows down by the railroad bridge and in winter they raced down Cook's Hill on homemade sleds.

There were days of fun and days of work. Learning to harness a horse and teaching a calf to drink from a pail as well as mowing the lawn and filling the woodbox were part of the life and training of a farm boy.

At the age of eleven, Herbert went to live with another uncle, Dr. Minthorn, at Newberg, Oregon. This uncle had founded a Quaker Academy at Newberg and Herbert Hoover continued his Quaker education. When Dr. Minthorn moved to Salem, Oregon, and opened a land office, his nephew helped him as an office boy.

As an Engineer

The pattern of his future life was set when he met a mining engineer. Encouraged by his new friend, he enrolled at Stanford University in California to study geology and mining. After graduating in 1895, he was hired by a British mining firm to open up new mines in Australia, then by the Chinese government to head their department of mines and railways. At the age of twenty-five, Herbert Hoover had established a reputation for being a top engineer with great ability for organization. He became very wealthy as he supervised mining operation all over the world.

His Humanitarian Work Begins

He was in London in 1914 when the first World War broke out. As Americans tried desperately to get home, they found Herbert Hoover quietly making arrangements for them, helping them to get their money exchanged and securing passage home. His first publicity in Iowa came as a result of this gesture. *The Des Moines Register* carried a story telling that Herbert Hoover had been born in Iowa.

As the German armies violated the neutrality of Belgium by smashing across it to get into France, Belgium was left destroyed and starving. Herbert Hoover was appointed head of a commission for collecting and distributing food to the people of Belgium. With quiet efficiency he managed to get more than a billion dollars worth of food and supplies through the blockade. He won the respect of the entire world for the honest, efficient work he did in Belgium.

When the United States entered the war, President Wilson, impressed by Hoover's work, appointed him Food Administrator. His efforts to save food and to increase production were so successful that the United States fed not only herself but all of Europe as well. Following the war, the Allied governments asked Hoover to head a Relief Commission, whose task was to feed the countries of Europe that had been ruined by the war. His activities covered twenty-three countries. In 1921, famine and disease broke out in Russia. The Soviet government appealed to Mr. Hoover for help. More than twenty-three million tons of food were delivered in Europe during and after the war.

Many times Herbert Hoover used his own personal fortune to be sure that food supplies got through. He never accepted any salary for the services he performed, not even later when he became President.

As President

He had a lifetime of accomplishments behind him by the time he was nominated for President in 1928. West Branch was in the headlines of the papers across the nation when he announced his intention of beginning his campaign in the place of his birth.

On election day, the nation honored him by putting him into office with a landslide vote. He carried all but eight states. The whole world acclaimed the election of this great humanitarian as the President of the United States.

As Iowa and the world rejoiced at his inauguration in March, 1929, the future looked bright. This man who had done so much to relieve suffering and starvation in the world was being honored with the highest office America could bestow. It seemed a fitting reward for one who had offered so freely of his time and money. Few could see at that moment that he was headed for trying times, that the Great Depression was only eight short months away.

Although business was booming when Hoover took office in 1929, there were some warning signs. For one thing, the purchasing power of the farmer had dropped. Having expanded his farming operations during World

War I to feed all of Europe as well as the United States, he now found himself with surpluses for which there was no market. The farmers, therefore, could not take their share of manufactured goods off the market. Also there was a slowing down in industry. More cars were being manufactured than there were people buying them. The steel industry, taking its cue from the car manufacturers, slackened its pace. There was also less construction of houses, buildings, and highways.

A few cautious bankers were beginning to become concerned. Too many people were buying cars, houses, radios and refrigerators on time payments. If industry slowed down too much, people might be laid off work, and they wouldn't be able to meet their payments. Also, bankers had loaned money to investors to buy stock. Of course, as long as the stock market kept going up there was no cause for concern. However, there was a little nagging worry about the price of stock going down instead of up.

The stock market crash came in October, 1929. By November, the value of stocks had dropped by thirty billion dollars. Suddenly, America became afraid. Confidence in American business was swept away. People were afraid to lend; businesses were afraid to expand. Banks began to fail. The list of unemployed became longer and longer. By 1932, fifteen million people were out of jobs.

When it became evident the depression was getting worse, President Hoover and the Congress acted to stem the downward trend. The Federal Farm Board was instructed to buy up agricultural surpluses. A public works program was initiated. The government loaned money to banks, industry, railroads and insurance companies to save them from bankruptcy.

It was not enough. The depression lengthened, sprawled across the land, and laid its heavy hand on every state.

The election of 1932 came during the months when the depression was the worst. As Herbert Hoover entered the White House on a wave of popularity, so in 1932 he was defeated. On election day there was a landslide, but it went the other way. Only six states voted for him. He and the Republican Party went out of office blamed for the depression.

As Elder Statesman

With the passage of time, Iowa and the rest of the nation restored him to his rightful place in the pages of history. Grateful foreign nations made countless awards and presentations in their appreciation of his humanitarian work done in their countries. Fifty-eight colleges and universities gave him honorary degrees. His advice and counsel was sought by Presidents Truman and Eisenhower as well as leaders of other countries. As an elder statesman, from his seventieth year on, his counsel was sought on everything from governmental reorganization to world affairs.

In 1951, the State of Iowa made plans to give an Iowa Award. The first one was given to Herbert Hoover. Placed in the gateway to the Hoover Cottage in West Branch, it reads:

> To Herbert Hoover
> President of the United States
> Native Son of Iowa
> Citizen of the World
> Statesman
> Humanitarian
> Engineer

270

Herbert Hoover Library at West Branch

Administrator
Who has worn the world's greatest
Honors with humility
The State of Iowa grants
The Iowa Award.

Today the tiny cottage in West Branch has become a national shrine. Restoration work was begun by the Hoover Birthplace Society, and the twenty-eight acre area surrounding the cottage became the Herbert Hoover Birthplace Park. To the side of the cottage is the restored blacksmith shop and across the creek is the Statue of Isis. This statue was given to Herbert Hoover by the school children of Belgium.

In 1962, the Herbert Hoover Library was dedicated. It was established to preserve the papers, books, and mementos of the President and to make them available to students for study and research. In addition to the large collection of papers, the Library has exhibit rooms containing gifts from people and countries all over the world. Diplomas, citations, and awards presented to him line the walls.

271

President Hoover came back to West Branch, August 10, 1962, on his eighty-eighth birthday. The Library was dedicated that day. President Truman joined President Hoover in West Branch to share in the dedication. As the two presidents stood side by side on the platform, President Truman stepped away to allow President Hoover to receive alone the love and respect of his fellow-Iowans.

His death

On October 20, 1964, West Branch received word that Herbert Hoover had died in his New York City apartment at the age of ninety. His burial would be at the place of his birth. The entire nation mourned the passing of this man who had won the respect and admiration of the entire world.

As President Johnson proclaimed a thirty-day mourning period, he spoke of Hoover as "a gentle and tolerant man who will long be remembered for humanitarianism, humility, courage, and the strength of faith which motivated his action."

Iowa's Governor Hughes said in a statement: "The story of Herbert Hoover is the story of the fulfillment of the American Dream, in which any boy of humble origin can, through hard work and diligence, enjoy the best the world has to offer. Mr. Hoover went one step farther. He gave back to the world, selflessly and tirelessly, the best he had to offer."

General Eisenhower said of Hoover: "He has by his great service earned the gratitude of America and the entire world. Everywhere, he was known as a friend of humanity."

President Truman said: "He was my good friend and

I was his. As a devoted public servant, he will always be remembered for his great humanitarian work."

On a cloudless Sunday afternoon, as a late October sun splashed through the scarlet and gold of the autumn trees, Iowa said farewell to its most famous and revered son. Burial took place on a grassy knoll overlooking the Hoover cottage and the Hoover Library. As he had been reared in the stark simplicity of the Quaker faith, so in death he returned to that heritage. The pomp and splendor that attends the funeral of a chief of state only served to heighten the quiet dignity of the Quaker graveside rites.

Herbert Hoover never escaped the influence of his Iowa heritage. At the end of his life he returned to his people.

Chapter 26

THE FIVE SAILOR SULLIVANS

It was a strange looking craft for the Cedar River, an old flat-bottomed rowboat with a torn sheet waving gaily in the breeze for a sail. Aboard, five little boys and one big dog looked with wonder as they slowly drifted from shore and out into the middle of the river channel.

"Everybody bail!" shouted George, the oldest and leader of the crew. The miniature sailors fell to, scooping up the water from the bottom of the boat with tin cans.

"It just keeps leaking in!" gasped Matt breathlessly.

"Yea," chimed in Joe, "it's coming in faster than we can bail it out."

"Abandon ship!" ordered the lanky leader. Obediently the boys and the dog hit the water with a resounding splash.

As George reached the muddy bank of the Cedar and scrambled ashore, he turned to check on his crew.

"Hey! We forgot. Al can't swim!"

In the middle of the river, Al, the baby of the crew, was thrashing wildly at the water. Before the crew could jump into the water, the dog, as if sensing the danger to his small master, paddled over to Al. The tiny boy wound his fingers in the dog's thick mat of hair and hung on. Slowly the dog swam down the river with the current, angling carefully toward shore.

The other boys ran along the river bank, shouting encouragement to little Al and calling to the brave dog. In a few minutes they had the child and were pulling him in to the safety of the shore. The homemade ship bobbled in the current downstream and sank to the muddy bottom with a gurgle.

Mrs. Thomas F. Sullivan did not hear about the escapade with the homemade ship for several days, but when she did, she lined up her five little boys and said sternly, "Now you boys promise me. You are never to set foot in a boat again. Understand?"

The five little boys nodded solemnly in agreement.

The Attack on Pearl Harbor

Landlocked as Iowa is, in the very middle of the Middle West, one would not expect the great oceans to beckon its young men. But during World War II it was Iowa that gave to the world one of the greatest examples of loyalty and sacrifice in the annals of American naval history—the five Sullivan brothers of Waterloo.

The five brothers—George, Francis, Matt, Joe, and Al—were seated around the radio that Sunday afternoon in December of 1941 with their sister and father and mother.

Mr. Sullivan was a railroad freight conductor on the Illinois Central Railroad out of Waterloo. It was a peaceful, quiet Sunday, and Father Sullivan looked with pride on his five strong sons, now almost grown men, and thought fondly of the scrapes and struggles he had gone through to raise the lively group.

They had been good boys, fond of the outdoors, spending their Saturdays fishing and hunting along the banks of the Cedar River, which flowed through the very heart of the little midwest city of Waterloo. George, the oldest, was always the leader and spokesman for the five. The rest accepted his position without question, down to Al, who was always considered the tag-along by the other four.

Suddenly the quietness of that Sunday afternoon was broken by the terse announcement from the radio: The Japanese are bombing Pearl Harbor!

The boys listened in amazement. George and Francis had already served a "hitch" in the navy. Some of the ships that were being bombed at Pearl Harbor were familiar names to the two brothers.

"The *Arizona!*" shouted George. "That's the one our pal is on!"

When the first shock of the Japanese attack on the American base was over, Iowans, as all Americans, knew that they were now a part of the great war that had been raging in Europe.

"Well, I guess our minds are made up, aren't they fellows?" announced George, still assuming the leadership for the brothers. "And when we go in we want to go in together. If the worst comes to the worst, we'll all have gone down together."

The Sullivans Stay Together

The United States Navy Department did not favor having five brothers all assigned to the same ship, but George wrote a letter to Washington stating that they would all join the Navy if they could stay together. The

276

Navy needed young men at once and reluctantly agreed to the unusual request.

By the early months of the next year the five brothers had been assigned to duty aboard the *USS Juneau,* a light cruiser. By May they had taken part in a trial patrol run in the Atlantic and returned for a short leave. Mrs. Sullivan's prized possession was a picture of her five sailor sons taken on board the *Juneau.*

The *Juneau* soon left the east coastal waters and sailed into the Pacific. A few letters trickled back from the boys. They could not write too often, but every letter that Mrs. Sullivan received during those first discouraging months of the war ended with the cheery message, "Keep your chin up."

During the last days of November of 1942, the *Juneau* was engaged in the thick of a fight centering around the Solomon Islands in the Pacific Ocean. All through the night preceding November 28, the ship had been under attack; but with the first streaks of dawn, the Japanese attack lessened. The *Juneau,* slightly damaged in the battle, steamed wearily away from the battle zone toward home port. From somewhere a Japanese torpedo swished through the water. The *Juneau* exploded, throwing particles of steel high into the air. In a matter of seconds the huge ship disappeared into the ocean depths.

Mr. Sullivan had just picked up his lunch pail, ready to leave on his regular run on the IC when the message came that Iowa's five Sullivan brothers had been lost at sea. Sadly Mr. Sullivan took his lunch pail and went to work. Railroads must run if wars are to be won.

Never in the history of the American naval records had one family made such a great sacrifice for their country. Once during the Civil War, a Boston mother,

Mrs. Lydia Bixby, had lost five sons on the battlefield, The great Abraham Lincoln had taken time from his busy war duties to write her a letter of sympathy which has long been famous. President Franklin D. Roosevelt wrote to Mrs. Sullivan expressing his sorrow at her loss. But Mother Sullivan did not allow herself time to weep.

Mrs. Sullivan and the War Effort

The United States was losing battles in 1943. More men and more supplies were needed if the country was to survive. It was Mother Sullivan who provided a rallying cry to the nation. Bravely she offered her services to the war effort. During the next few months she appeared at defense plants, shipyards, bond rallies, and patriotic gatherings. "Keep working," she would plead. "We must work, give, live, and, if need be, die to make our country live. In that way my five boys will still be fighting." She spoke to more than a million American workers in 65 different cities, urging them on to greater sacrifices.

Iowa, along with her sister states, heeded Mrs. Sullivan's plea. Food from the rich Iowa soil poured out to the world from Iowa farms and "Victory" gardens. Farmers, spurred by the war effort, sought new ways to improve the soil through chemicals, devised machines to conserve man power, and developed high producing seed varieties to feed the armies of the Allies.

Industries in Iowa changed over to the manufacture of products necessary for the war. Munition plants sprung up where once Iowa cornfields had waved. Women began to perform tasks that had always been considered man's work. College campuses became a part of the national officers training program for the armed services. The Woman's Army Corps was formed and established a training center at Fort Des Moines just outside the capital city. Inspired by the example set by the Sullivan brothers, Iowa boys flocked to enlist in the armed services and served in every theater of the world-wide war front.

When the long years of the war had dragged to a close, Iowa faced the new era of peace. Over 262,000 Iowans had served in the great War; over 8,000 had given their lives for their state and country.

Honored by Iowa

In honor of the five sailor Sullivans, the Navy commissioned a sleek new destroyer and christened it the *Sullivans,* the first ship to be named after more than one person. The *Sullivans* saw action in the Pacific area during the closing years of the war and engaged in duty during the Korean War. The Congress of the United States established a living memorial to the five Iowa brothers by planting a cluster of apple trees on the national capitol grounds.

The city of Waterloo set aside an eight-acre park in the very neighborhood where the Sullivan boys lived and played and named it "Sullivan Park". The park stretches along the same IC railroad line where Mr. Sullivan worked for 39 years. A shamrock plaque of bronze, taken from the deck of the destroyer *Sullivans,* stands in the center of the park, just a few yards from a tall straight elm tree which the Sullivan boys had planted when they were small. Sullivan Park is a reminder to all Iowans of the part their state played in World War II. Not far away the Cedar River flows quietly by.

Iowans Lead the Big Parade

The years following World War II were years of prosperity and social progress. They were marred by neither a depression nor serious unemployment. Living standards reached new heights. America came to grips with post-war problems both at home and abroad. Problems at home included one with transportation as growing numbers of cars on the road increased. Another was with education as schools became ill-equipped to handle the ever-increasing school population.

At the same time, scientific research brought changes

Des Moines Art Center

in American society. Agricultural scientists brought plants and livestock into increased yield and productivity. Industrial scientists created new products to further the comfort and ease of living for the American citizen. Space scientists opened new vistas as America awakened to the realization she need not be earthbound.

The cultural interests of Americans broadened and deepened as the arts began to assume a new proportion in American thought. America and the fulfillment of the American Dream were being reflected in the music, paintings, poetry, and literature of the artists.

Iowa became a center of both science and art. The University at Ames produced top agricultural scientists. The University at Iowa City, while maintaining law and medical schools ranked among the best in the United States, also produced a writers' workshop that is world renowned and space scientists making discoveries as significant as the discoveries of Columbus in an earlier age.

Chapter 27

IN THE ARTS

As the Wapsipinicon River winds its way between the rolling hills of eastern Iowa, it passes a tiny deserted town, clustered beside an old limesone quarry. Iowa was young when this little town was flourishing with an opera house, church, store, stone bridge, and Mr. Green's twenty-room stone mansion atop the highest hill.

Stone City was destined to give the world more than its rock and stone. Long after the quarry was exhausted, the church and opera house fallen into disuse, and the mansion crumbling on the hill, two Iowa artists found inspiration from Stone City to influence the world: Grant Wood, the painter, and Paul Engle, the poet.

Grant Wood was an Iowa farm boy. He had often wandered along the banks of the Wapsipinicon, studying the wild birds, watching the farmers as they plowed their fields on the neighboring hills, and marveling at the sweep of the land down to the quiet flowing river. Perched on a wood fence on his father's farm, he spent hours with a piece of charcoal and a scrap of cardboard sketching the chickens and the barns, the cows and the fences, the trees and the pasture land.

Behind him on a small slope sat his farm home, a two story white frame house with red barns nestling beyond. Everything the boy saw was a picture to be drawn. Fences were to be drawn on; walls to be scrawled on. On the stone basement wall of his father's home he had inscribed:

Grant Wood was born here, Feb. 13, 1891

When the boy was ten years old, his father died. Mrs. Wood and her four children were forced to move from the farm near Anamosa to the neighboring city of Cedar Rapids, but the memories of his early life on an Iowa farm never left Grant Wood.

In Cedar Rapids, Mrs. Wood struggled to support her family. The three boys helped by doing odd jobs for the neighbors, mowing lawns, and helping out with the work on the farms surrounding. When Grant was in the eighth grade, he drew a picture of some oak leaves and won a prize in a national art contest sponsored by a crayon company.

After he graduated from high school, Grant worked around Cedar Rapids as a general handyman. He made jewelry and was even a watchman in a funeral parlor. When he was 23, he bought a lot on the edge of the city and built a tiny shack where he lived with his mother and sister, Nan. Money was scarce. Often Grant was forced to trap rabbits for food. When World War I came, he joined the army, but always he was drawing pictures. He drew portraits of his fellow soldiers, charging 25c for an enlisted man and $1 for an officer. When the war was over, he returned to Cedar Rapids and became an art teacher in the public schools.

He made several trips to Europe to paint and to

study art. Returning from his last trip, he remarked to one of his friends, "All the really good ideas I ever had came to me while I was milking a cow. So I went back to Iowa." Grant Wood began to paint the scenes of Iowa which he knew so well: farmers in overalls, women in aprons trimmed with rick-rack, chickens, threshers eating dinner, Arbor Day at a country schoolhouse. Soon other painters were following his example, and a new trend in modern art was started, a return to the American scene.

Grant Wood could never forget the little deserted town of Stone City that he had known so well as a boy. Through the assistance of some of his friends he was able to open an art colony beside the Wapsipinicon in the little quarry town. Students flocked to Stone City to study under him. To house the artists, Grant obtained several old ice wagons from the city of Cedar Rapids, painted them gay colors and used them for bunks for the students. One of Grant Wood's most famous paintings is of Stone City.

One day, while in the little town of Eldon in Wapello County, he saw a house that attracted his attention. He took an envelope from his pocket and sketched the house with its pointed windows. Years later he used the house as the background for his famed "American Gothic" painting, portraying an Iowa farm couple. For models he used his dentist friend as the farmer and his own sister, Nan, for the woman.

The Iowa farm boy artist left his mark on many walls besides the basement wall of his boyhood farm home. His paintings today are coveted possessions of many art collectors, and his murals adorn libraries, colleges, and high schools throughout Iowa.

At the time Grant Wood was working at odd jobs

285

trying to finish high school, Iowa's foremost poet was born in the same city—Cedar Rapids. Like Grant Wood, the feel of Iowa was embedded deep within this sensitive boy. The youngest of four children, Paul Engle, early sensed the magic to be found in words. Christmas was truly Christmas when the gifts were books to be read. The boy grew up in the artistic culture that was fourishing in Cedar Rapids during the early decades of the century.

One day when Paul was in junior high school, the artist Grant Wood visited the eighth grade art class and demonstrated how he could paint the sound of music on canvas. But Paul Engle could fashion words to express the feeling of the music. Iowa's poet grew "a water-watched and river-radiant child", glorying in the restless beauty of the cornfields, charmed by the quiet flow of Iowa's streams.

Engle's studies took him to the east and then abroad as a Rhodes scholar before he returned to his native Iowa as a teacher in the State University. Within the shadow of the Old Stone Capitol, Paul Engle developed the SUI Writers' Workshop into a gathering point for many of the leading poets and writers of the nation. According to one critic, "Paul Engle has done more for the young poets and writers of this nation than any other person in America."

The literary world came to listen with respect to the poetic voice of Iowa's Engle. His poems have found their way into the leading literary publications of America, into school literature textbooks, and libraries throughout the nation.

Iowa's Storyteller

While Iowa's poet was growing up in Cedar Rapids,

a restless little boy with the skinniness that goes with being ten years old was sending the *Webster City Freeman-Tribune* skimming across the front porches of his hundred paper-route customers. Like many paper boys, Mack Kantor had a dog—a yellow dog named Trixy—who knew the route as well as his barefoot master. Money was not plentiful in the Kantor home, and after Mack had given his mother 74c from his paper route profits, he sometimes had as much as 25c for himself.

MacKinlay Kantor and his sister, Virginia, lived with their mother and the MacKinley grandparents in Webster City. In spite of being raised in a fatherless home with money often a problem, Iowa's future author found excitement, joy, and security in his Webster City childhood.

Like every boy, Mack Kantor loved to play cowboy, Indian, and particularly soldier. The boys of the neighborhood formed an army company, marched and paraded, fought and set up camp, built army barricades, and carried on attacks. Bombs were wood ashes which they hurled across the enemy lines.

From his grandmother, who could remember events of the Civil War period, and from his mother, who had an eager interest in American history, MacKinlay first learned something of the excitement of the events of the past. As a boy he often played along the Boone River timber where Sidominadotah, Inkpaduta's brother, had roamed and eventually met his death at the hands of the white settler, Lott. In Webster City there were some old pioneers who had joined the expedition from Fort Dodge to rescue Abbie Gardner from Inkpaduta's Scarlet Band. And for a young inquisitive boy there were always the old timers who loafed on the park benches and were always willing to relate their experiences in the Civil War.

During his grade school years, his mother obtained a job as reporter on the Webster City newspaper. When Mack was older, he helped his mother edit the paper. He grew up to be a foreign war correspondent in World War II and in the Korean War.

It is small wonder that from such a background that the Iowa boy went on to become the great story teller that he is today. His historical novel *Andersonville,* concerning the infamous prison camp of the Civil War, won for him the 1956 Pulitzer prize in literature. His more recent *Spirit Lake* is based upon Iowa's historic event, the Spirit Lake Massacre.

The Music Man

While Iowa's story teller was delivering his papers, not too many miles away in Mason City, a bright-eyed little boy was unwrapping a new flute he had ordered from a catalog. For many days he had waited for the postman to deliver the precious package from Chicago. No one in Mason City played the flute; in fact, the boy was not too sure just what a flute looked like. When he had torn away the wrappings and examined the shiny new instrument, he discovered that he had to hold the flute sideways to play it. He was about ready to wrap the flute up and send it back, but he decided it would be too much bother, so he kept it.

The boy's mail order flute was to lead him on to become one of the country's leading musicians, conductors, and composers. A boyhood spent in Iowa was an important part in the making of Iowa's Music Man, Meredith Willson.

Although music and song played an incidental part

in the growth of the state during the first century, Iowa did not produce anything in music that was distinctively Iowa. Dvorak, a noted Czech composer, did spend some time during the middle 1800's visiting in the little northeast village of Spillville. Many think it was in this quaint little community that the composer derived inspiration for his famed *New World Symphony,* but the themes of the work are Czech, and not truly Iowan. It was left for a young Mason City boy with a flute to catch the gay spirit of Iowa life.

As a child, Meredith Willson hated to practice his piano lessons on the big, black upright piano, but bands —they were something different. Parades, circus bands, the town band—these provided the thrills of his boyhood. Someday he too would play in a band.

His first appearance behind footlights, according to Meredith Willson's own account, was when he was six years old. The local theater was presenting a play that called for children, and little Meredith donned a frog suit and hopped around the stage. For this performance he was given a penny, which he promptly spent at the local Candy Kitchen.

The boy learned to play the instrument well. The summer after he was a freshman in high school he was accomplished enough to play the flute with an orchestra that had been hired for the season at the Lake Okoboji resort area. He was a member of his high school orchestra, and when he graduated, he wrote a song for his senior class.

The young flutist left Mason City as soon as he graduated and set out for New York to study flute. He played in theater orchestras, John Philip Sousa's Band, and finally with the New York Philharmonic Symphony Orchestra.

As he rose in musical circles, he became musical director and conductor for many radio and TV programs as well as for several motion pictures. But it was the Broadway musical comedy *The Music Man* that let the world share the love and enthusiasm that Meredith Willson has for his native Iowa. Through its lilting music runs the happiness of the boy who spent his childhood in a small Iowa town.

Iowa has now grown old enough to have a story of its own that can be told only by Iowans whether it be in painting, poetry, story, or song. Today the world is listening to such Iowans as Grant Wood, Paul Engle, MacKinlay Kantor, and Meredith Willson.

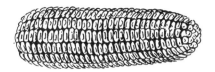

Chapter 28

THE IOWA WALLACES

One April day in 1862, a young minister could be seen sloshing his way through the ankle deep mud of an Iowa road. The Mississippi was flooding; the river at Burlington was ten miles wide. In order to avoid sinking in over his ankles in the sticky clay, the young man resorted to walking in the grass along the side of the road.

"The soil here must be good," the Reverend Henry Wallace was thinking as he walked along, bound for his first preaching assignment in Iowa. He could feel the grass, thick under his feet, springing back as he lifted his heels.

He stopped and looked around as he reached the top of the knoll. He saw hills covered with groves of elm, hickory, and maple. In the gentle slopes between were patches of blue-green meadow grass.

"Grass like that doesn't grow unless the soil is mighty good," he repeated to himself.

In his mind, the young minister was already thinking about owning some fertile, Iowa farm land.

Henry Wallace's first call was to preach in two churches: one in Rock Island in Illinois and one across the river in Iowa at Davenport. The arrangement did not prove satisfactory, for the churches were jealous of the amount of time the minister spent with the other congregation. It was not long before the Reverend Henry Wallace became a controversial figure.

Feelings were running high in the United States in 1863. President Lincoln had just issued his Emancipation Proclamation, and some northerners did not agree with the President. Iowa had some Southern sympathizers living in Davenport. Some of them were leaders of the town and members of Henry's church.

Nonetheless, when the President asked for a day of fasting and prayer following the Emancipation order, the Reverend Wallace decided to take a firm stand. He preached a sermon from his pulpit favoring the Proclamation. He called attention to the corruption in a nearby military camp and spoke of business men in Davenport who were making money from the corruption. From then on, opinion was divided in Davenport concerning the Reverend Henry Wallace.

A precedent was established, however, that day in Davenport. The Wallaces spoke out for what they believed to be right, regardless of what the consequences might be.

Farmer and Journalist

Following the Civil War, much cheap land was still available in middle and western Iowa. Henry Wallace made his first land investment with $1000 borrowed from his father. To begin with, the farm was to help out on his income, but it became an exciting thing to make money by buying and selling land. By 1877, when he

A covered bridge in Madison County

resigned his ministry and moved to Winterset, the family owned three farms in Adair County.

It was at Winterset where the Wallaces had their first taste of journalism. Henry Wallace missed his pulpit from which he could express his view. Persuading the local editor to allow him to write a page on agriculture, he was never again without a sounding board. He soon bought a paper of his own. He wrote of dairying and cultivating, but mostly he wrote about grass. "Land will wear out," he warned his readers, "unless it is put back to grass."

By now, people were beginning to recognize his wisdom. They called him, affectionately, Uncle Henry. His articles were being printed in more and more midwestern newspapers. In 1883 Uncle Henry was asked to become editor of the *Iowa Homestead* at a salary of $500 a year. He continued to live in Winterset, writing for his own paper and mailing his articles to the *Homestead* office in Des Moines.

"Harry" Wallace

The Wallace's oldest son, Henry C. Wallace, was a student at Iowa State College at Ames in 1886. Not being particularly interested in attending school, he was casting longing eyes at his father's rich farm land. When a tenant on a 300-acre farm gave notice, "Harry" received permission to take over the farm. Henry C. was being called Harry to keep from confusing him with his father.

Harry soon discovered that life on a farm can be delightful, but it can also be lonely. He had fallen in love with a girl at school, but she was from the East. He was afraid to ask her to marry him. He felt sure she would not want to live on an Iowa farm. He was most surprised to find her accepting his proposal of marriage.

The Wallace household was much like that of any farm family in Iowa in the 1880's. There was a greater interest in national and world affairs, more books and magazines, more interest in music and art, but the isolation was the same. Visiting the neighbors was the extent of social events. The tenant house was cold and it had no conveniences. It was in this tenant house in October, 1888, that Henry A Wallace was born.

Henry A. Wallace

The stay on the farm ended abruptly when Young Henry was four years old. His father had been asked to return to Iowa State College, complete his degree, and accept a position as Assistant Professor. The family rented a small, run-down house on the outskirts of Ames and moved in 1892. They had almost no income while Harry was trying to crowd two years' schooling into one to become an Assistant Professor. After that, it was a little easier. They had his salary of $1300 a year.

While at Ames, Harry became a partner in publishing a small paper, *The Farm and Dairy*. Most of the articles he wrote were reports of experiments being conducted on the college farms and in the classrooms.

Meanwhile, Young Henry was beginning his education. He was taught to read by his mother. He helped her with the plants in the garden. He was getting to know other people besides his family as their home was visited by associates and students of his father. One student interested him more than all the rest. He had become a welcome visitor in their home. He was a Negro. His name was George Washington Carver. The friendship between the six year old Henry Wallace and the Negro continued throughout their lifetime. Henry Wallace later said his interest in breeding corn came partly because the great scientist Carver had taught him an appreciation for plants in a way he would never forget.

While this Wallace family lived in Ames, problems for Uncle Henry were piling up. He was using the editorial page of *The Homestead* to level criticism at the policy of the railroads and business. He felt that these groups were taking undue advantage of the farmer, and that it was his duty to point this fact out. In February, 1895, he was asked to leave.

Wallaces Farmer

Grandfather Wallace without a paper was not fit to be lived with. Hastily, the Wallace family met to seek an answer to the problem. Could the little paper *The Farm and Dairy* be the solution? They approached Harry's partner to see if he would be willing to sell his share to the Wallaces and he agreed. And so it happened that the little paper at Ames took a new name: *Wallaces'*

295

Farm and Dairy. By the end of the year the paper was moved to Des Moines and was published weekly. The name was changed to *Wallaces' Farmer* and a motto appeared across the top of the front page: Good Farming——Clear Thinking——Right Living.

Wallaces' Farmer became as essential as the Bible in the homes of Iowa farmers. Besides news of farming it enlarged to include a chatty woman's page and the weekly Sunday School lesson. Farm children all over Iowa bounced along over the dirt roads in the Sunday surrey, reading their Sunday School lesson from *Wallaces' Farmer.*

Professor Wallace resigned his position at Iowa State College in 1896 and moved his family to Des Moines. He devoted full time to being business manager for the family paper. Young Henry was eight years old when the move was made. His father bought ten acres beyond the outskirts of the city and built a house on it. This is where Young Henry grew up.

Henry's duties at home were that of a farm boy. Feeding the chickens, milking cows, feeding the livestock and working in the garden formed the basis of his work and of his pleasure. His mother was constantly after him to change his clothes before he went to school "so he wouldn't smell like a farm boy", but appearance meant little to Henry A. More and more, his mind was on the plants he was growing in the soil of their ten acres.

A New Kind of Corn

He followed carefully the opinions of his father and grandfather as they were written in the family paper. He read the bulletins published by Iowa State College. He watched, with consuming interest, the experiments

Wallace's findings established a new frontier in corn raising

being made with corn, and he did not agree with the conclusions that were being reached. Too much emphasis was being placed on the beauty of an ear of corn. A pure strain, Henry had noted, did not necessarily mean it was the strongest. The way an ear of corn looked might not have anything to do with the way it might yield.

Henry began his own experimenting. He took thirty-three ears of corn that had won in a Corn Show and used them to plant five acres of the family acreage. While other boys were hunting, fishing, and playing ball, Henry was planting, thinning, cultivating, and finally detasseling five acres of corn. It was back breaking and exhausting work, but his findings established a new frontier in corn raising. The yield varied from thirty-three to seventy-nine bushels to the acre, and the ears that looked the best turned out to be the lowest yielders. His experiments, carried further, led to the development of hybrid corn.

Following graduation from Iowa State College in 1910, Henry A. Wallace continued his experiments with corn. He was writing for the family paper now, as a reporter and as an editor, but his experiments with corn continued. He was looking for a hybrid that would consistently outyield any other corn, not in the controlled conditions of a laboratory, but in the heat and drought and wet of a cornfield. Corn breeding became his all-consuming interest.

He did take time out to court a girl, although his method seemed a little strange. The story is told in the Wallace family of Henry's taking a book about agriculture in China with him on dates and reading it to her. But in 1914, when he had saved $2000, they were married.

World War I came to America in 1917, and with it Herbert Hoover was appointed Food Administrator. In order to erase the shortage of fats in Europe, Hoover asked for an immediate increase in hog breeding. Young Henry was appointed to Hoover's Hog Price Commission in November, 1917.

American agricultural production went into high gear, and even with the signing of the Armistice there seemed to be little reason to cut back production. There were so many underfed people in Europe crying for food and clothing, surely the American farmer would be called upon for years to continue high production. The truth, however, was far different. By 1920, *Wallaces' Farmer* predicted a farm depression unless some method of control of production was devised.

"Harry" in Politics

After twenty-six years as editor of *Wallaces' Farmer*, Harry Wallace accepted the appointment of President Harding to become the Secretary of Agriculture. Moving to Washington in March, 1921, he took office about eight months after the farm depression had struck. By May, the purchasing power of the farmer was 78% of what it had been before the war. Secretary Wallace asked the President to call a meeting of farm leaders to examine the problems of agriculture and to suggest some solutions. But very few people in the still-prosperous East agreed that there even was a problem. President Harding was inclined to agree with this. The only plan to pass Congress was to make more money available to banks so the farmer could borrow more. Secretary Wallace knew the real problem was over-production, but no one would listen. By 1923 hog prices were lower than they were before the war. Then, just when Secretary Wallace's opinions were gaining favor, President Harding died.

Henry A. in Politics

In 1929, the depression became general. In 1932, President Franklin D. Roosevelt was elected with a promise of a New Deal. This included, he said, help for the farmers, and he was asking Henry A. Wallace of *Wallaces' Farmer* in Des Moines to help him carry out his promise. Thus young Henry was called to Washington to hold the same office his father had held.

The inauguration took place on March 4. By March 10, the opening meeting of a farm conference was in session. Action to solve the farm problem was underway. The farmer, at long last, had a voice speaking for him in Washington, the voice of Henry A. Wallace.

Eight years later, President Franklin D. Roosevelt reached out his magic wand to touch Henry Wallace. As the third term tradition for President was broken by Roosevelt, Wallace became Vice-President of the United States.

In 1944, President Roosevelt did not name his running mate. The decision was made at the Democratic Convention for Harry Truman to be Vice-President for Roosevelt's fourth term. The fourth term, however, was less than four months old when the President died and Vice-President Truman became the President. Henry A. Wallace had missed becoming President by three and one half months. He worked as Secretary of Commerce in Truman's cabinet for a year and a half and resigned.

He never again entered politics successfully nor did he return to live in Iowa. Running an experimental farm at Salem, New York, he returned to his first love. At his farm he continued his corn experiments and did research on the cross-breeding of chickens. He followed world events closely until his death.

The Wallaces were never people to stay put, either in their job holding or in their thinking. The grandfather felt too restricted in the pulpit and became a farmer, then an editor. Although love of the soil was paramount in the lives of all three, they needed a place to air their views. The family paper was used by all three for this purpose. The father and son took further opportunity in positions in the government. None of them learned the art of politics. They were too blunt, too independent in their thinking for that. But in their honest, forthright attempts to make known to the rest of the country the problems of agriculture, they reached their greatest area of usefulness.

Chapter 29

ROSWELL GARST—CORN
DIPLOMAT

Iowa became the center of international attention one day in September of 1959.

President Eisenhower had invited Nikita Khrushchev, Premier of the Russian Soviet Union, to visit the United States. Mr. Khrushchev had replied that he would accept the invitation, but that one of his stops on the proposed coast-to-coast tour must include a visit to the Roswell Garst farm at Coon Rapids, Iowa.

At first the governmental officials in charge of the Premier's visit were puzzled. Where was Coon Rapids and who was Roswell Garst?

Coon Rapids, located on a bend of the Middle Raccoon River in Carroll County, was a tiny frontier settlement when Roswell Garst's grandfather, a Civil War veteran, rode into town to open up a general store. The store flourished as the pioneers rushed into the rich central plains to homestead the new land. By the time

Roswell was old enough, he too, went to work helping his father and grandfather in the family store.

Groceries and dry goods did not interest the young boy. He was more fascinated by the rich black soil and the lush grain and pasture lands that covered the gently sloping hills around Coon Rapids.

When World War I broke out, Roswell Garst was studying agriculture at the University of Wisconsin. He returned to Iowa to raise food for the war effort on a 200-acre run-down farm that his father owned on the edge of Coon Rapids. From that day on, the family store held no interest for the young man.

As the young farmer plowed the land, planted the seed, and harvested his crop, he kept thinking about ways whereby a farmer could produce more food at less labor. One day he heard about a new type of hybrid seed corn that Henry A. Wallace and his father, Henry C. Wallace of Des Moines, were developing. He made a trip to the capital city and obtained some of the new seed. When he saw the full golden ears that grew from the strong stalks, he decided to produce and market the corn. In the midst of the depression, Garst founded a seed company, which today produces 5 per cent of all the hybrid seed corn planted in the United States.

Roswell Garst held open house on his farm to show his neighbors the benefits of his discoveries. He found that by fertilizing the new seed, using insecticides to keep out pests, and by mechanizing as many farm operations as possible that he could increase his farm yield with less labor.

A group of Soviet farm experts touring the United States in 1955 heard about Garst and his farming methods. They asked if they could visit Coon Rapids. Mr. Garst felt that it was his duty to help all people in the

Roswell Garst of Coon Rapids

world improve their way of living. After he had taken the Russians on a tour of inspection of his farm, the visitors invited Mr. Garst to visit them in Russia. This was an unheard-of event at that time, for Americans were not encouraged to visit in the USSR.

That fall, Mr. Garst went to Russia. He visited Premier Khrushchev and his wife at their vacation place on the Black Sea. The two men spent their time discussing and comparing Iowa and Russian farms. Before Roswell Garst left, he had sold the Soviet Union a large quantity of his hybrid corn seed, given the Russians information on how to improve their agricultural program, and in turn invited the Khrushchevs to visit his farm in Coon Rapids.

Another delegation of Russian farm experts visited the Iowa farm that fall. Later a Rumanian delegation came to study the efficiency of Iowa farming methods. Many people in the United States criticized Mr. Garst for his close associations with countries behind the iron curtain, but the Iowa farmer only replied that feeding people was good politics as well as good business.

On September 23, 1959, Premier Nikita S. Khrushchev, himself, arrived in Iowa. In his own account of his visit, Krushchev wrote, "After a warm meeting with the governor of the state, we went out of town to the cornfields, so dear to my heart. And I must tell you that the Americans know how to grow corn. We enjoyed the lavish hospitality of our host, my old acquaintance, Mr. Garst, who arranged an interesting meeting with farmers for us."

Roswell Garst showed the Khrushchevs his farm and entertained the Russian couple at a fried chicken dinner at the farm home.

Mr. Garst returned to Russia again in 1962 and again shared his knowledge of farming with Soviet farm experts as well as agriculturists from other iron curtain countries.

Although Khrushchev has now retired from the Russian political scene, many of Russia's farm methods of today are based on the advice of Iowa's international farmer, Roswell Garst. For many years this man has been dedicated to sharing with others his knowledge of good farming methods. In his blunt, folksy manner, he maintains that a plentiful food supply is the only way to peace.

"For the world to spend 100 billion dollars a year preparing for a war that nobody wants—nobody expects and that no one can survive—is not less than global insanity," states Mr. Garst.

For many years Roswell Garst was disturbed by the piles of wasted corn cobs piled out in Iowa farmyards to be burned and destroyed. Always ready to try a new idea, Garst tried grinding the cobs for cattle feed. He discovered that his cattle thrived on the food. A new era in cattle feeding was opened.

"America must use its food surpluses for peace." His most recent suggestion is to finance poorer nations so that they can buy the grain surpluses of America and raise chickens. "To live in the 20th century, one must be educated, but it's almost impossible to educate a hungry person."

Recently Mr. Garst toured Central and South America on a government sponsored tour. He talked to farmers, looked over their corn and cattle, and made his typical recommendation: good seed, good chemicals, and let the farmers see the results.

Today Roswell Garst is one of the world's largest producers of hybrid seed corn. He owns 2500 acres of farmland near Coon Rapids and manages 8000 additional acres. His farm business is one of the most efficient and profitable farming operations in the world and has served as a model for the agricultural programs of many other nations.

Perhaps of even greater importance is the fact that an Iowa farmer, in the middle of a cold war, helped open up an exchange of ideas between the two great powers of the world: Russia and the United States.

Chapter 30

VAN ALLEN OF THE SPACE AGE

"We are now approaching the Van Allen Radiation Belts."

Such an announcement coming over the inter-com of a space ship might greet a traveler of the future as he returns to earth from a trip to the moon. The outer radiation belt resembles a huge doughnut encircling the earth 8,000 to 12,000 miles out in space. The moon traveler will pass through the inner belt when he is about 3400 miles from earth, but within twenty minutes, going at the speed that it will be necessary to travel to and from the moon, the ship should be through the belts and settling down to earth again.

These radiation belts, invisible to the human eye, will prove to be landmarks to future space men, just as the Atlantic and Pacific Oceans were landmarks to the earliest explorers. These belts, called the Van Allen Radiation belts, bear the name of a small town Iowa boy —James Van Allen.

How did it happen that an Iowa boy gave his name to one of the most important discoveries in space?

James Van Allen was the second boy in a famliy of four boys born in the little Henry County seat town of Mount Pleasant. His father was a lawyer; his mother an Iowa farm girl. Mr. Van Allen taught his boys the importance of hard work in accomplishing the things that were to be done. He felt that every waking hour should be spent in doing something useful. He expected his boys to study hard and bring home good grades from school. When the boys were not busy in school, they were assigned chores to do around home such as chopping wood or caring for the lawn. James started to school when he was four years old. Most of his classmates towered over him in size, but not in his school work.

James Van Allen's favorite subject in high school was physics; in fact, he was so interested in the subject that his teacher almost had to push him out the door at night so he could lock up the school. Often the boy would spend many hours figuring out a problem that no one else in the class could solve; he would always stick to it until he had found the answer.

The Van Allen home was situated on a quiet corner of the little Iowa town. The house had been owned by the Van Allen family since 1866; in fact, the Van Allens and Mount Pleasant had grown up together. Sunday afternoon the citizens of the town would often see the Van Allen family taking a quiet stroll around the neighborhood. There was the lovely campus of Iowa Wesleyan College—and of course, the famed Harlan House.

The Harlan House had been the home of Iowa's senator during the Civil War period. Senator Harlan's only daughter had married Abraham Lincoln's only liv-

James Van Allen was the second boy in a family of four boys. From left to right, Dr. Maurice W. Van Allen, Judge George O. Van Allen, Mr. William A. Van Allen, and Dr. James A. Van Allen.

ing son, Robert Todd Lincoln. Many of the older townspeople could still remember when the three Lincoln grandchildren had come to visit their Grandpa Harlan. The senator had stood them up against the door of his house and marked their height in the wood. Then, as today, the Harlan House was a treasured landmark of the town.

Like his older brother, James Van Allen, after graduating from high school, enrolled at the local college. In the vine covered physics building on the Iowan Wesleyan campus, he measured the cosmic rays, tracked meteors, and made a magnetic survey of the town. As a freshman, James worked with his college physics professor, Dr. Thomas C. Poulter, on equipment that was used on Admiral Richard Byrd's Second Antarctic Expedition on which Dr. Poulter acted as chief scientist.

During World War II, James Van Allen served as ordnance and gunnery officer in the United States Navy and designed a new type fuse. He was then sent out to the Pacific to instruct the men on the use of the new invention. From this he learned how to pack many delicate instruments into a small space.

In the European theater of the war, the Germans had been making great advances in rockets. During the attacks on Britain, many German rockets were launched from the French coast to land in England. When the first German rockets were captured, Van Allen was called in to study their construction. The Space Age had arrived, and James Van Allen was on hand to pioneer the new frontier.

Van Allen sent rockets loaded with research equipment high into the upper atmosphere. He designed a "rockoon" whereby a balloon would lift a rocket high in the air and have it fire by a radio command from a ship.

After the war, Van Allen returned to his native Iowa as head of the physics department of the University of Iowa. He continued to study outer space by launching Skyhook balloons, which carried apparatus high into space. Many of these Skyhook balloons were launched from Iowa, but it was unsafe to send up large ones. The Coast Guard provided ships, and Van Allen was off to Greenland to launch his research rockoons from there.

It was Van Allen who guided the construction of cosmic ray equipment in the first American satellite. James Van Allen was fast becoming one of America's most outstanding young scientists. It was Van Allen equipment in Explorer I that measured the bulge of the equator.

But the excitement came when Explorer III started sending back to earth strange, confused signals. What was wrong? James Van Allen sat up most of the night trying to decipher the strange messages from the Explorer's tapes. Slowly the truth dawned on the young

310

scientist. There must be layers of radiation surrounding the earth far out in space. They were probably made of material thrown off the sun and trapped by the earth's magnetism. They were radiation belts. One writer has explained the belts as being like two moats around a castle, guarding the earth, with a drawbridge at each pole. As the belts dip downward at the poles, the particles in them hit the earth's atmosphere. That would explain the northern lights. The discovery of the radiation belts was a most important step in space exploration.

Now his research took him all over the world: Spain, the Arctic, the Antarctic, Hudson Bay, down to the equator. The door had been opened on space. Man could now expect many contributions from space research: long range weather forecasts, aids to navigation, improved radio and TV communication, and new knowledge in biology and medicine.

One spring America's foremost space scientist attended his class reunion in Mount Pleasant. Half seriously, he invited his class to celebrate their 50 th class reunion with him on the moon. Such an event is fast becoming a possibility as Van Allen and his young scientists at the University of Iowa continue to carry out their research in space.

Perhaps the best formula for boys and girls who dream of becoming space scientists is to pattern their efforts on the life of James Van Allen: good grades, hard work, careful research, and persistence.

UNIT IX

Changing Patterns

In 1964 the Supreme Court ruled that all Congressional Districts must have the same number of voters. This was brought about because of a population shift in the United States. There were several reasons for this. One reason was the migration of people from rural areas to urban centers. As farming became highly mechanized, the need for farm workers grew less. Farming became big business as it became impossible to operate a small farm profitably. The small landowner sold his farm and these farms were combined into large ones where new types of farm machinery could be used. Thus the population became centered in some parts and sparse in others.

This condition brought on the need for the reapportionment of the state legislatures as well as the National Congress. Iowa found its population shifting, and by the 1960's a plan had to be devised to make it possible for people to receive their rightful amount of representation.

The population shift also reflected a change in industry. The trend that started after the Civil War picked up speed in the twentieth century. The United States had begun as a farming nation, but by 1960 less than 10% of the population was engaged in farming.

Chapter 31

MEET THE GOVERNMENT

The chartered bus wheeled out of the Des Moines traffic and eased into the parking lot. It had been a long ride and David was glad of a chance to step out and stretch his legs.

He looked down at the city sprawled out before him and then turned to the state capitol building which loomed behind him. His eye followed the long wide flight of steps up to the big double doors and on up to the shining gold dome that was reflecting the morning sun with a dazzling brightness.

"It's big!" exclaimed David. "Can I climb up to the dome?"

"We'll see how good your legs are after we've finished our tour," laughed Mr. Miller.

Mr. Miller had chartered the bus for the trip to the Iowa State Capitol. The class had just completed a unit on Iowa history. "We'll just call our trip to Des Moines the final test," Mr. Miller had announced, and of course

Iowa State Capitol at Des Moines

all the class had agreed that a trip to Des Moines was a wonderful way to take a unit test.

David could see as he approached the big building that the capitol was built in the form of a huge rectangle with a towering gold dome in the center and four smaller domes that seemed to button down the corners. Above the main entrance tall Corinthian columns supported the heavy roof.

"It's made of stone. All different kinds of stone," observed David.

"Most of it is Iowa stone, too," added Mr. Miller, "from around Anamosa."

David paused for a moment to gaze up at the group of bronze statue figures. An old pioneer was peering off into the west with his trusty scout beside him and an Indian nearby. A Civil War cannon mounted on the steps pointed menacingly from the entrance. Far to David's right, out on the captiol lawn, rose a tall granite shaft.

315

"That's the Soldiers and Sailors Monument," explained Mr. Miller. "It was built to honor the men who fought in the Civil War. See the statue of General Crocker of the Iowa Brigade up there?"

"And he's sitting on Beauregard!" David would have liked to examine the statues that adorned the side of the monument, but Mr. Miller was already holding open the heavy door to the capitol building.

The high ceilings, the long halls with their great windows, and the soft murmur of voices which issued from the open office doors filled David with a strange feeling of awe. The inside of the building was arranged in the form of a cross with halls running off into four directions. A grand rotunda extended from the top of the dome down through the center of the capitol to the basement story. The walls were made of marble, granite, and various woods from Iowa's forests: walnut, butternut, cherry, oak, and catalpa. David wanted to go over to the brass railing which surrounded the rotunda and peer up toward the dome, but Mr. Miller was guiding the class over to an impressive office. Above the door was the seal of Iowa, displaying the state motto: "Our liberties we prize and our rights we will maintain."

"Is this the Governor's office?" David was impressed by the dignity of the large reception room.

"This is it," reassured Mr. Miller. Turning to the lady at the reception desk, he asked, "Is the Governor in? We have an appointment."

The class was ushered into the office of the Governor. The Governor stood up smiling.

"Good morning. Allow me to welcome you to your state capitol. I understand you have come to find out about your Iowa government."

"Yes, Governor," added Mr. Miller. "The class and

316

I thought that the best way to learn how the state is run was to visit and see for ourselves."

"Well, I think you are most wise, and I think the Governor's office is the best place to begin."

"This is the Governor's chair," the Governor began. "The person who sits in this chair represents the head of the Iowa government. As Governor, I am a part of what we call the *executive* department of your government. *Executive* means that we take care of the business of the state and enforce the laws of Iowa."

David slid his hand across the polished desk top.

The Governor continued. "You will see many officials of the State of Iowa during your visit today. Many of these people are elected by the voters, but there are many other people working here that are not elected, but are appointed by me to their jobs."

"How do you get to be Governor?" David asked.

"To be a Governor of Iowa, a person has to be an Iowan for two years and be at least 30 years old. That means that you young people will have to wait a few years before you can sit behind this desk. I hold my office for two years. I am elected by the people of Iowa in November of every even-numbered year."

"Perhaps the class would be interested to know where you live, Mr. Governor," suggested Mr. Miller.

"I live here in Des Moines in the Governor's Mansion on Grand Avenue. No doubt you will see my house when you take a tour of the city. I might add, too, that the Governor is the commander-in-chief of all the state military forces. I make recommendations to the General Assembly for the good of the state. I, in turn, have the right to approve or reject all the bills that the Assembly passes. And, of course, I am called upon to make speeches and appearances throughout the state."

The members of the class could see that the Governor was a busy man, for there were already several people out in the reception room waiting to see him with pages of important looking papers tucked under their arms. Mr. Miller thanked the Governor for talking to the class. The Governor shook hands with everyone and ushered them from the office.

Across the hall from the Governor's office, the class saw another office. Above the door in gold letters was the sign "Secretary of State." Just then the superintendent of the capitol building and grounds came over to the sightseers.

"You must be the class I agreed to show around this morning," he said. "Is this your first visit to the capitol?"

"Yes, sir," answered David.

"Then perhaps we had better start here on the main floor." The class followed the man down one long hall after another. The halls were lined with more offices: Auditor of the State, Treasurer of the State, Attorney General, Lieutenant Governor. As they walked down the hall, David saw several tattered and faded battle flags behind their tall glass showcases.

"All of these offices along here, with the Governor, make up the executive branch of our Iowa State Government. They, like the Governor, are all elected for two years. The Lieutenant Governor is the next most important man to the Governor. In case the Governor cannot serve out his term, the Lieutenant Governor becomes the Governor. The Lieutenant Governor also acts as the President of the Senate. We'll see the Senate Chambers upstairs in a few minutes.

"The Secretary of State keeps the records of the state," went on the guide. "The Treasurer keeps track of the money; the auditor checks on the Treasurer's books, and the Attorney General acts as the official lawyer for the state."

The superintendent led the class down one hall and opened a double door for the students to look inside.

"Now these are the Supreme Court Chambers. The men who work here make up the second department of our state government—the *judicial*. You can remember that along with *executive*, can't you? *Judicial* sounds sort of like *judges*. And that is what the Supreme Court is—a group of nine judges. It is their duty to rule on the laws of Iowa which the General Assembly passes."

The room looked like a courtroom with a long table and nine sturdy chairs.

"Now we'll go upstairs," announced the superintendent.

As they crossed to the grand stairway that covered the entire side of the building, David stopped to look up into the huge dome with its statues and paintings. Down below people were milling around in the basement cafeteria.

"Now up here on the second floor, we meet the *legislative* branch of the government. *Legislative* means the part of the government that makes the laws of our state. As in most other states, we have two houses or two parts that together make up the General Assembly. Come over here and we'll go into the Senate Chamber first."

The class went up a small flight of stairs into a circular meeting room filled with desks. At the front of the room was a long desk mounted high above the other desks.

"This is the Senate Chamber. You see each senator has his own desk and a desk for his secretary. Perhaps you can find the names on each desk. All the counties of

The Legislature in action

Iowa are grouped into senatorial districts, and each senator is elected from a district. A senator is elected every four years. Can you find the desk of your senator?"

"And let's not have anyone in the class asking me what our district is," warned Mr. Miller.

The class moved about the room, stopping over each desk to read the name carefully. In the far corner of the room they located the desk that belonged to the senator from their district.

"One of you may sit at the desk, if you wish. Now say that you were a senator, and that there was a bill up before the Senate stating that all school vacations should be extended to six months instead of the customary three."

The entire class shouted their approval at this suggestion from the capitol guide.

"You would probably want to vote 'yes' on such a bill. If you were voting in the House Chamber, all you would have to do would be to press a little electric button, and your vote would be registered up on the electric counting board. When all the votes were counted, the bill would be on its way to becoming a new law for Iowa. Now you can see why the General Assembly members—the Senate and the Representatives—are called the law makers."

The superintendent pointed to the raised desk in front. "The President of the Senate sits there and presides over the meetings. He is the Lieutenant Governor, as I told you downstairs. Just behind him are the seats for the newspaper reporters, and up in the balcony are seats for visitors. When the Senate is in session, any one can come in and attend the meeting."

The class then crossed the hall, past the rotunda, and entered the Chambers of the Representatives. There were many more desks in this room.

"There are more members in the House," said the guide. "House members represent nearly equal numbers of citizens. Some of the smaller counties have now combined and have one House Member representing them. Other counties, where the population is much larger, have many representatives. Polk County has the largest population and the most representatives. The Representatives are elected for a term of two years."

As the group left the Chambers of the Representatives, the guide pointed to a room nearby. "This is the Iowa State Law Library. With its 150,000 volumes it is one of the largest and most complete law libraries in the United States. It is for the use of the judges of the Supreme Court and other governmental officials as well as the public.

"I suppose no visit to the capitol is complete without

a climb to the dome. When you reach the top, you can see out over the city of Des Moines. You can walk around on the inside of the dome and see down to the bottom floor of the building. The dome of our State Capitol is one of the larger domes in the world. It is a long climb, but I'm sure the view is well worth it."

After David had climbed the seemingly endless winding stairs up to the dome—618 steps in all—and down again, he was ready to rest on a bench in the hall and watch the other sightseers and the office workers who were bustling from office to office.

"Are you all ready for one more long walk?" asked Mr. Miller.

Down more flights of stairs the group went until they reached the basement floor. Mr. Miller turned a corner, and David saw a long hall with a small door at the far end.

"This is a tunnel which leads from the capitol building over the Robert Lucas Building. You see, Iowa has outgrown its capitol. It was necessary to build other buildings to take care of all the people who are needed to attend to the business of our growing state. This tunnel is about two or three blocks long and saves workers from having to go out of doors when they have papers and letters to deliver to another department."

The class started through the tiled tunnel.

"It surely takes a lot of offices to run the government of Iowa," observed David.

"Yes, indeed it does," answered Mr. Miller. "The buildings of our state government are spread over 93 acres of land right here in the heart of Des Moines. But we must remember that when we think of our Iowa government that there are 99 courthouses spread across Iowa where the business of the counties are carried on.

And besides all these, there are hundreds of other buildings that house town and city business."

As the class reassembled on the main floor of the capitol, David saw a desk with brightly colored pamphlets on it. The woman behind the desk smilingly offered David a pamphlet. On the cover was displayed the Iowa flag: three vertical bars of red, white, and blue with the American eagle carrying a streamer on which was inscribed the Iowa motto. Just below the eagle, in bold red letters, was the word *Iowa.*

While Mr. Miller was busily counting to see if everyone was present, David glanced inside the pamphlet. There was a picture of the Seal of Iowa, the official state bird—the eastern goldfinch, the state flower—the wild rose, and the official state tree—the oak.

"All aboard!" shouted Mr. Miller as he stood at the front entrance and motioned the class toward the waiting bus.

The bus moved out into the stream of traffic flowing past the capitol grounds. Mr. Miller and his class were just one of the hundreds of school groups that tour the State Capitol grounds each year to witness, first hand, their Iowa State Government in action.

Chapter 32

IOWA TODAY

Iowa still retains much of the loveliness and charm that first impelled Marquette, standing in the prow of his tiny canoe, to exclaim with delight, "This is the place."

Driving across Iowa today, however, one can see that the state is changing. Road signs along Iowa's borders announce: "Iowa—where factory and farm share prosperity." This was not true two or three decades ago. Where once family farms adjoined rural villages, there are now sprawling factories and abandoned farmsteads. This condition is similar to the change which the United States once experienced. For the first hundred years of its existence, the United States was a rural nation. During its second century the country changed into the urban nation that it is today. As Iowa enters its second century of history, a similar change is taking place.

Iowa faces the future

Change in Farming

Iowa's history began with the fur traders, but soon the early frontiersmen were rushing in to homestead the cheap land. Iowa soon became established as an agricultural state. The two World Wars created a shortage of man power on the farms and forced the farmers to seek labor saving devices. Farming became mechanized. Where formerly a farm family lived and worked on a farm of 10 to 160 acres of land, one farmer, today, can handle as much as 260 acres without working too hard. This increase in efficiency has come about because of new farm machinery which allows one man to do the work of several, because of new and improved techniques in soil conservation and farm operation, and because of the increased production possible from highly developed seed and modern chemicals.

As farms become larger and machines take over the more laborious work, the number of farmers decreases

325

and the average size of farms increases. The small family homesteads are taken over by the larger farms. In the change, the small farmer has been forced to leave his land to seek employment in the factories of the larger cities.

Increase in Industry

Since farming still remains a big business in terms of employment and dollar value, industry is necessarily centered around agriculture. Iowa industry concerns itself mainly in three areas: the processing of farm products, the production of goods for the farm markets, and the extracting of raw materials.

The processing of Iowa's farm products makes up the bigger part of Iowa's manufacturing. Iowa's packing plants, located in Sioux City, Ottumwa, Cedar Rapids, Waterloo, Mason City, Des Moines, as well as several other smaller towns, are its most important industry. Iowa's butter, cheese, and ice cream are well known exports. Cedar Rapids and Clinton have two of the world's largest corn products factories, manufacturing corn sugar, corn oil, starch, and glucose. The Quaker Oats Company of Cedar Rapids is the largest cereal plant in the world. Many plants scattered throughout the state can sweet corn, beans, tomatoes, asparagus, and cucumbers. Various waste products from corn are used in the manufacturing of insulation. Dressed and frozen poultry, raised and processed in Iowa, are shipped all over the world.

Nurseries were established in the early years of the state in southwestern Iowa to supply the early pioneers with seed before they crossed the Missouri River for the western lands. Today nurseries in towns such as Shenandoah ship their stock to all parts of the nation.

The manufacture of farm equipment and products for the use of the farmer forms another large part of Iowa's industry. Corn pickers, tractors, combines, and hay balers find a ready market within the boundaries of the state. The largest tractor manufacturing plant is located at Waterloo. Washing machines are produced at Newton, fountain pens at Fort Madison, and the Alcoa Aluminium Rolling Mills of Bettendorf are the largest in the nation. Woodworking plants are numerous in Iowa. Their products consist of doors, window frames, molding, ready-cut houses, venetian blinds, and furniture.

Iowa is not particularly rich in minerals, but the manufacturing and processing of what minerals are available make up the third area of industry. Iowa ranks third in the nation in the production of gypsum products. This deposit of gypsum is found in a 50 square mile plot near Fort Dodge. The processing of portland cement, plaster of paris, and house plaster in Iowa is second only to the state of New York. Mason City is often called the "brick and tile capital of the world."

Iowa has other industries, of course, which are not directly dependent upon farming: plants that manufacture pleasure boats, travel trailers, lawn mowers, small gasoline engines, trampolines, chemicals, and such varied industries as the button plants centered in Muscatine and the Collins Radio Corporation of Cedar Rapids.

Printing and publishing make up a notable part of Iowa's industry. Such plants range from the small town weekly newspaper to the nationally known *Des Moines Register and Tribune*. Des Moines has long been the agricultural publishing center of the United States with such publications as *Successful Farming* and *Wallace's*

Farmer. Meredith Publishing Company of Des Moines is the largest publishing house, producing *Better Homes and Gardens* and *Successful Farming.*

Out-of-state industry has recently shown a trend to locate their factories in rural villages where labor is plentiful and factory sites are relatively inexpensive. Perhaps one of the most attractive features for industry in Iowa is the large surplus of farm labor available with mechanical skills and aptitudes. At present about one-fifth of the state's population is supported by manufacturing.

Population Shift

Job opportunities on Iowa farms are decreasing, but job opportunities in manufacturing, commerce, and service establishments are increasing as Iowa moves toward a more industrial culture. This industrialization of Iowa has caused a rapid population shift in Iowa which has taken two forms. First, there is the noticeable population shift *out* of Iowa to other parts of the United States. From 1950 to 1960, enough people moved out of the state of Iowa to make a city the combined size of Des Moines and Marshalltown. Of these 230,000 native-born citizens who left Iowa, most of them were from 21 to 44 years old who were seeking a job or a better position.

Besides this out-shift of population, there has been an *inner* shift from the rural areas of northern and western Iowa, swelling the population in the city areas of southern and eastern Iowa. The new factory buildings tend to cluster in an area bounded by Fort Dodge, Mason City, Dubuque, Clinton, Keokuk, and Des Moines, with the one exception of the urban development along the Missouri River at Sioux City and Council Bluffs.

Here the job hunters have been able to find employment in the many industries of Iowa.

This movement from the farms and small towns to the city has had a marked effect on the small villages of Iowa. Most of the small towns that dot the Iowa countryside grew up as farm trade centers. With the automobile and the truck, the farmer has been able to make frequent trips to neighboring cities, robbing the small town of much of its trade. The small town, though decreased in population, still continues to survive in Iowa because the farmer must still rely on its closeness for such necessary services as provided by the grocery store, gas station, doctor, school, and church.

As Iowa cities increase in population, the city stretches out into the surrounding rural area. The city workers seek out an acreage where they can enjoy the freedom of country living and still be within commuting distance of their jobs. Sometimes factories as well move into the farm area to take advantage of the space for their operation. Soon the rural area has become a part of the expanding city.

Effect of the Population Shift

As the population of Iowa shifts, many phases of life are affected. The one-room schoolhouse for every four sections of land has been replaced by the large modern centralized town school, offering a higher quality of education at minimum tax cost. The country church has all but disappeared from the countryside as congregations feel the pressure to centralize and reorganize for more effective service. Government, too, has felt the change from rural to urban. Counties which are principally rural and do not support many industrial plants are making plans to consolidate their county government into one central courthouse to serve several counties. State government, too, has been forced to draw new lines for equal representation in the state legislature. This was accomplished by combining several counties into one district where population was decreasing and allowing the faster growing counties to have more legislators.

Wide ribbons of new 4-laned highways crisscross Iowa, providing trucks with fast efficient routes to deliver the produce of farm and factory. To feed these main arteries of the highway system, Iowa has more surfaced roads per square miles of area than any other state in the nation. Railroad lines, particularly in the rural counties, are fast being abandoned, and all that is left in many small towns to remind the citizens of the once busy freight lines of the railroad era are empty depots with their brown paint peeling in the sun. Fast growing city areas boast modern commercial air terminals making it possible for Iowans to embark by air for any part of the world.

As the face of Iowa changes, the attitudes of Iowans are changing too. Iowa has long been known for it middle-of-the-road attitude on most questions. Even as late as World War II, many Iowans felt strongly that their state and nation should remain isolated from world entanglements. But with the new industrialization, a new voice is being heard in state politics and government— the voice of Labor. Iowa is being led away from its former rural conservatism as the urban population gains in influence. But beneath it all the Iowan still clings stubbornly to his state's motto: "Our liberties we prize, and our rights we will maintain."

The Future of Iowa

"In all that is good, Iowa affords the best," boasted one noted Iowa slogan maker. Today Iowa has over 380 public libraries, more than 500 newspapers, 66 radio stations, 14 TV stations. 100 state parks and 137 public hunting grounds preserve many of the scenic areas and natural beauty spots of Iowa. The State Conservation Commission plan, over the years, has been to provide state parks so that no Iowan need be more than 25 miles driving distance from a state recreational area. Caves, lakes, plots of unbroken prairie land, forests, historic sites are protected and reserved for public use.

In the future Iowa can look forward to becoming a more urban society without losing its position in the nation as a leading agricultural state. Iowa will continue to contribute its part in the scientific research for the fast developing space age. With her program of state conservation, Iowa's natural beauties will continue to lure the vacationer to its many lakes and streams. Her artists will continue to be heard as they interpret for the world the culture of Iowa's people.

Iowa is in a period of rapid change. As she faces her second century as a state, she is assuming an important position in science, industry, education, music, literature, and art. But in spite of the changing times, Iowa fields will continue to dominate her fertile acres and produce the food for the markets of the world.

Acknowledgments of Source Material

Benjamin F. Gue, *History of Iowa* (Volumes I-IV); Federal Writers' Project of WPA, *A Guide to the Hawkeye State;* Barbara S. Yambura, *A Change and a Parting;* Irving B. Richman, *Ioway to Iowa;* Johnson Brigham, *Iowa—Its History and Its Foremost Citizens;* Cyrenus Cole, *I Remember, I Remember;* Cyrenus Cole, *I Am a Man—The Indian Black Hawk;* Marshall McKusick, *Men of Ancient Iowa;* Everett Dick, *Vanguards of the Frontier;* Shirley Thomas, *Men of Science;* Hanry Sabin, *The Making of Iowa;* Bruce E. Mahan, *Stories of Iowa;* T. P. Christensen, *The Hawkeye State;* John E. Briggs, *Iowa Old and New;* Jessie Merrill Dwelle, *Iowa Beautiful Land;* Department of Anthropology, *Documentary History of the Fox Project;* Cyrenus Cole, *A History of the People of Iowa;* Bea McNamara, *The Okoboji and Spirit Lake Massacre and Kidnapping Story,* Abbie Gardner, *The History of the Spirit Lake Massacre;* Russell Lord, *Wallaces of Iowa;* A. A. Hoehling, *The Fierce Lamb; Waterloo Courier, Glidden Graphic, Iowan* Magazine, *Annals of Iowa, Palimpsest, Journal of History and Politics, Chicago Tribune* Magazine Section, *Iowa Official Register,* Lewis-Hill manuscripts in Minnesota Historical Association Building, Zebulon Pike *Journals,* Lewis and Clark *Journals,* Diary of Jane Bicknell courtesy of Mrs. Hortense Heyhood, Judge George O. Van Allen of Mount Pleasant, Iowa State Social Welfare Office of Des Moines. Meredith Willson, *There I Stood With My Piccolo.*

Index

337